Robert

I hope you
Enjoy the
book

THE PUCK STOPS HERE.
MY (NOT SO) MINOR LEAGUE LIFE

Written by Bruce Landon

Copyright 2019© Bruce Landon • All Rights Reserved • ISBN# 978-1-7323545-3-1
No part of this book may be reproduced, stored in a retrieval system or transmitted in any form or by any means, electronic, mechanical, photocopying, recording or otherwise, without prior written permission of the copyright owner or the publisher.

Written by: Bruce Landon
Ron Chimelis, Wayne E. Phaneuf and Joseph Carvalho III, Editors
Book Designed by: Michelle Johnson and Curtis Panlilio
Printed by: Sheridan • Published by The Republican, 1860 Main Street, Springfield, MA 01103

In Loving Memory of
Tammy Jacobson Landon
November 20, 1975 - February 20, 2019

All proceeds from the sale of the book will benefit the Tammy Jacobson Landon "I Can Hear You" scholarship fund at Clarke School for Hearing and Speech.

Bruce Landon with his daughter Tammy. (Photo courtesy Landon Family)

DEDICATION

In the early morning of November 20, 1975 our second child was born, about six weeks earlier than what was expected, weighing 3 lbs., 11 oz. From her very first breath, until the last breath she took a little before midnight on February 20, 2019 she was loved by so many people.

Tammy Jacobson Landon passed away peacefully, surrounded by those who loved her so very much.

This book is dedicated to Tammy for so many reasons, but first and foremost is that she was my inspiration to take on this project at all.

A dad has a special bond with his daughter (or in my case, two) and I have always hoped that in addition to being a good father to both Tracey and Tammy, I was also a person they could talk to, no matter what it was about. Marcia, my wonderful wife and mother to these two beautiful children, was always there for them, through the good times and the bad.

Tammy and I shared many special moments. One sunny afternoon in May of 2017, shortly after I retired, we had a long and deep conversation and I shared stories with her that she had not heard.

"Dad you have to start writing this stuff down," she said. It was with her gentle prodding, and her ability to instill confidence in me, that I simply started writing, with no idea where it would take me.

It was a project I enjoyed doing, but it was a struggle at times. Every time that would happen, I would pick up the phone and call Tammy. I needed her reassurance to just keep writing. She would handle the editing and write a foreword for the book.

She had a degree in English and was an outstanding writer, so this was to be a father/daughter undertaking.

When Tammy was diagnosed with a very rare cancer on May 11, 2018, I put my work on the back shelf. Without Tammy I had no interest in continuing. About a month after she had finished her first chemotherapy treatment, we were sitting and just talking as I tried to comfort her.

The truth was that she was the strong one. She cared more about how her mom and myself were holding up, than her own health.

"Dad, just promise me that you will finish the book," she said.

Tammy was special in so many ways. She could make people giggle or laugh out loud. She cared about everyone around her and was a friend to so many people who touched her life.

She was a caring, giving person who loved family, her dogs, and was devoted to Stephanie, her wife. She left us way too early, but she also left many wonderful memories that we will always cherish.

When Tammy was nearing her final hours, Marcia, Tracey, Stephanie and I were around the head of her bed.

I reached over and gave her a kiss on the forehead, and said, "Tam, your dad finished the book." She looked at me with a little smile on her beautiful face.

This is that book. It is a promise kept. It is also the opportunity for readers to share our lives and her vision, which was the driving force in bringing it to fruition. The Landon family hopes you enjoy it, and we appreciate the time you'll invest to be part of our lives and that vision.

- Bruce Landon

FOREWORD

My first experience with Bruce Landon was no different than that of many people. He was a pro hockey goalie, playing for the Springfield Kings.

I was a teenager at the Eastern States Coliseum, sitting in an aging barn the American Hockey League team called home. A bunch of guys would figure out which one of us could have access to a car, and we'd be off to West Springfield to watch our team take on the hated Hershey Bears, Rochester Americans, or - if we could get tickets - the Providence Reds.

Watching hockey as a kid, I always related to the goaltenders, perhaps because I couldn't skate very well. Pro goalies must be excellent on their skates, of course, and so it was with Landon, but that didn't stop me from imagining it was me out there, making the kick saves or grabbing the high shot with my glove.

But that is not the Bruce Landon I have come to know. The man who wrote this book is one of intellect and complexity, confidence and self-doubt. He's one who spends more time than he'd probably care to admit, wrestling over what choices in everyday life or the bigger picture are the right choices, the better choices or the most honorable choices - but never the easy ones.

Bruce has gained enough recognition to have had a street named after him: Bruce Landon Way in downtown Springfield. It's only appropriate that he take a long look back to tell us how Bruce Landon's way led to Bruce Landon Way.

Bruce might be the only person I know who has not irked me by calling me "Ronny." With most people, the slang version of the first name comes off as patronizing, as if I were still that kid in the Coliseum stands.

But Bruce could call me Ron, Ronny, Hey-You or whatever and it would still represent a reference to friendship that makes me flattered and appreciative to be even a small part of his book. Working in media requires - or should require -

a certain detachment from the people you are covering, especially at the pro level, where friendships risk the compromise of objectivity.

Bruce never uses his influence or stature to gain an edge, though, and that opens the door for real communication - and comradeship.

Some years ago, a college coach in another sport was leaving one school for another that offered him much more money. Before he left, he said he would always remember his old school "like family."

That irritated me because responsible people don't leave one family for another family that pays more. I thought of Bruce Landon too.

That's because so many coaches and players talk about their teams as a family but treat them like a business. With Bruce, it was the other way around. He had to run a business but treated it like a family.

That helps explain why so many stayed with him for years and decades, even when some of those years were difficult. You'll meet many of those people in this book.

Throughout his management career, Bruce's biggest obstacles included fans like me - people who grew up at the Coliseum and falsely remember those years through rose-colored glasses, as if every night was played to capacity and every game was an epic. In their effort to win support, modern Springfield teams were competing against a romantic vision of the nostalgic past - but it was a vision that, to some extent, was just not true.

Let the record show that as of the 2017-18 season, only twice did Springfield hockey teams average more than 5,000 fans per game. Both of those were under Landon's management in downtown Springfield in the late 1990s.

Fond memories grow fonder as the years pass, and all of us whose first glimpse of Landon stem from his playing days should enjoy them. He does, too, but he always lived in the present.

He always thought the next game was more important than whatever happened in 1970. More than any other reason, that is why they still play pro hockey in Springfield.

When Bruce told me, he was writing a book about his years in hockey, as a player and then in all levels of management and ownership, I was skeptical at first. Writing a book is a big undertaking, though no bigger than the episodes and decisions in his life he wanted to describe.

My doubts were mostly whether they would interest anyone who was not like me, the fan who used to watch him play. But as his project has unfolded, I've become convinced it's a story many people would want to hear - a lifelong journey of triumph and doubt, celebration and disappointment, framed by lessons learned from a turbulent youth and an adult life that called on him to balance family considerations with professional dreams that carried no guarantees.

At this writing, I have been employed at The Springfield Newspapers for 35 years. Most of that time was spent covering sports, but relatively few were spent on the pro hockey beat. Like Bruce, I rarely if ever felt the urge to leave the Pioneer Valley, which is one reason I've always admired him, because he had many, many opportunities to do so.

You won't hear this from Bruce, but every famous person in pro hockey knows him and their respect is universal. My first suggestion was to pepper the narrative with name-dropping about guys like Gordie Howe and Wayne Gretzky, and maybe even ask some hockey legend to write this foreword as a way to grab attention.

Bruce wasn't interested because he's never been one to "grab attention." His philosophy has always been to earn whatever attention comes his way and accept not just the spotlight, but the responsibility that comes with it.

He's the most honest sports figure I encountered in 30 years of covering sports at high school, college and professional levels. This was not always to my advantage: for most of our professional relationship, his best information was off the record, which to a writer is what revealing a special sauce is to a chef - and then telling him he can't use it.

What he did tell me, though, was fact and not spin, regardless of whether we were on or off the record. On even delicate business matters, not once did he mislead me to improve his own circumstance, even temporarily. I don't think anyone who has not worked in media can understand how rare that is.

How Bruce kept hockey alive in Springfield for nearly 20 years after the Falcons were formed will always astonish me. As this book will tell you, the chances to bail out and sell were numerous, but finishing what he started demanded he find a way to keep the team in Springfield. Ultimately, he succeeded, and the Springfield Thunderbirds have been a marketing success.

Without Bruce Landon, there never would have been a Springfield Thunderbirds and the MassMutual Center would have lost its prime tenant years ago. Sometimes I wondered why he cared when so few other people did, and I empathized with him because I was sure that he asked himself the same question many times. You will find some interesting and even bizarre on-ice hockey stories in these pages, but this is not a play-by-play compilation of great games from years gone by. The vast bulk of it is behind the scenes. All of it is very personal, more personal than many of us (including me) might share.

What surprised me most in this autobiography was how often Bruce got into fights and scrapes, and showed his temper in ways that might sound a little rough. Knowing the standards to which he holds himself, I even find it hard to believe, but if it's Bruce Landon saying it, I believe it.

I also believe you will enjoy this book, whether you're a hockey expert or not. It comes from the memory and also the heart, which always make for the most interesting reading.

Most of all, it's an honest book that reflects the honesty of a man's career in hockey and in life. Having known Bruce for decades, I thought I knew all there was to know about him, only to learn how much there was that I didn't know

This has been my opportunity to learn those things and learn about the hockey business as it's evolved and changed since those long-ago days when I sat in the Coliseum seats, making those kick saves in my dreams. This is your opportunity, too. Enjoy, for I can assure you, it will be time well spent.

- Ron Chimelis
Columnist, Springfield (Mass.) Republican

INTRODUCTION

Why write a book? Who am I to think I have anything to say that anyone outside of my immediate family (and even that could be questionable) would want to read?

I have no idea what the Dear Lord has in store for me, so I try not to look too far ahead. I do recall one time, I was sitting at my computer in my downstairs office, listening to some Elvis Presley music and collecting some thoughts on what I might write about. It might have been a little easier to concentrate if my wife would have shut off the vacuum.

Many times, during my playing career and then in my management days, something would happen, and I would always hope I could remember it. It soon became my standard line that when I would tell a story, I'd say, "It's in the book."

Or would be, anyhow. This is that book, the one I was talking about.

I never had any aspirations of really writing a book until I made the decision to retire. I was never concerned about staying active physically, because I am always doing something.

However, I was worried about what I was going to do to keep myself mentally sharp. My mom suffered from dementia and then Alzheimer's disease. The more research I did, the more I found out that as you get older, you need to find a way to keep your brain busy - and I was not into crosswords or Sudoku.

This book has nothing to do with ego. I did not go into it with visions of book signings or seeing it in the discount aisles. It is simply all the memories of a senior citizen who spent a lifetime in all levels of hockey, challenging his memory and sharing some hopefully interesting stories of that life.

These pages draw from my recollections of things from the past. It wasn't about research, statistics or game scores. When I started the project, it was not supposed to be the Bruce Landon story, but more about everything that came into my life, personally, in my years of professional and amateur hockey. It's intended to bring readers behind the scenes with stories I always thought were funny or sad, or perhaps just informational.

If anything, I hope that it may make you just say or think - what the hell, did that really happen? Most of all, I hope you enjoy revisiting my experiences with me, not for my benefit but to get a better understanding of the joys, disappointments, challenges and decisions I faced in my life, as have countless others in my profession and of my generation faced.

- Bruce Landon

TABLE OF CONTENTS

Dedication 5
Foreword 7
Introduction 11
2. The Landon Family 15
3. The Early Years 25
4. Minor Hockey and the Junior Years 27
5. First Pro Camp 33
6. The Springfield Kings 37
7. Second Pro Camp 43
8. Return to Springfield 45
9. Marcia Landon – My Favorite Fan 49
10. Famous Coliseum Brawl 53
11. The New England Whalers 61
12. Retirement from Playing 77
13. The Worm Farm 85
14. Cooney Buys the Indians 87
15. My Run for AHL President 109
16. The Falcons are Hatched 111
17. Wayne LaChance 123
18. Springfield Pro Hockey LLC 127
19. Charlie Pompea Years 133
20. Coaches 149
21. Characters in Hockey 163
22. Affiliations 179
23. The Birth of the Thunderbirds 195
24. Closing 203
INDEX 215

Brothers Terry [L] and Bruce Landon [R]. (Photo courtesy Landon Family)

2
THE LANDON FAMILY

It makes some sense to introduce myself, so you know a little bit about my past. You should know how a crazy path of good luck, great salesmanship and a whole bunch of turns impossible to forecast - along with what I will admit was a lot of hard work - took me from 128 Yonge Street in Kingston, Ontario, to my "Broadway" next to the MassMutual Center - 45 Bruce Landon Way in downtown Springfield, Massachusetts.

We are all products of our past and our early experiences. They shape our opinions, values and goals. They help us determine what we consider important what we do not.

My own journey was no different.

The Landon family of Norm, Jess and my older brother Terry grew up in Portsmouth Village, located on the bay of Lake Ontario. Unlike today with its yacht club, waterfront condo development and new restaurants, Portsmouth was a tough neighborhood in the 1950s and '60s.

I still find it hard to believe our little stucco home, complete with an outhouse and no indoor plumbing, is now listed as one of the historical homes in the Village.

The house was adjacent to a store owned by two older women, Becky and Rose Silver. It was a combination grocery store and fountain bar and home to about 50 cats that you had to kick off the barrels of penny candy.

At one time there were far more than 50, but one Halloween night, a couple of my buddies and I got a little crazy. I have never fired a gun in my life, but I could shoot the crap out of a jackrabbit from twenty paces with my trusty pea shooter. I can't remember for sure, but there may have been some small firecrackers involved as well.

Bruce Landon's father, Norm Landon [L], in the Canadian Army. (Photo courtesy Landon Family)

I was not a good toddler. Throughout my entire childhood, mother used to say, "You are a rotten kid," and she'd give me a playful slap across the back of my head. More than once, I would run away from home, but a couple of hours later they would always find me in the same hiding spot - my neighbor's rhubarb patch.

I ran over to the lake so often that Mom eventually had to tie me to the clothesline that ran from the corner of the house to the outdoor toilet.

Saturday night was bath night, and Mom would pump the cold water into a big aluminum basin, then boil up some hot water to add to it. How hot it was depended on how badly I had behaved that week. On more than one Saturday night, I was putting my tiny, two-year old butt into freezing cold water.

Our house was also down the street from the Kingston Penitentiary, a maximum-security prison and home to some of the worst criminals in Canada. It did not happen often, but there were times when a convict would escape, and we would hear the siren go off.

When that happened, we had to go into lockdown, which for us meant hiding in the cellar. The Pen was also the first memory I have of where my dad worked. He was a prison guard and sadly, like most of his jobs over his lifetime, it did not last long.

Even today, some people are reluctant to believe beer drinkers can be alcoholics.

But they can, and Dad was a beer alcoholic who would guzzle down ten Molsons before lunch. Verbally and at times physically abusive to my mom, he also took out a lot of his anger on my older brother, Terry, by locking him next to the coal bin with the rats.

I was on the end of his belt buckle more than once, too, up until I was about 13. But it finally stopped after he chased me up the stairs and I turned and I told him, "you hit me one more time with that strap, and I am going to kill you when you are sleeping."

I certainly don't condone violence as an answer to domestic problems, but the incident shows how badly a home situation can become when abuse and alcohol are its controlling influences.

When he wasn't drinking, Dad did care about us and that's important to remember, too. Even though we could not really afford it, he moved us out of Portsmouth, which was not a particularly good place for kids to grow up.

In our case, we were hanging around with some really bad kids. Two of my childhood buddies ended up serving a lot of jail time. One of them, Johnny D., escaped prison with the help of his father and, for a long time, was on Canada's most wanted list.

The only reason my brother and I survived is that rather than breaking into cars or houses, we had turned to hockey.

Dad tried his best to follow my hockey career over the years. He made sure we got to our early morning practices and games. He did his best to buy us hockey equipment, even if he had to borrow money from others - something we found out later he did far too much.

But Dad was always broke, and more than once tapped my brother, Terry, with some sob story and a request for money. When I turned pro, I was given a $3,000 signing bonus and a day after getting the check, my old man called and asked if he could borrow $2,500.

He said he was behind on his mortgage payments, and I gave him the money. He must not have used it for the house, because shortly after I gave him the check, they lost the house and had to move to an apartment. He'd also promised to pay me back, but that never happened, either.

Dad died of a heart attack at age 65. My last time spent with him occurred when I drove up from Springfield for a visit. He was working in the Legion, a service club that catered to veterans. I sat at the bar for about an hour and he knew I was there, but he never came upstairs until someone told him I was getting ready to leave.

He sat down and we talked for two minutes. Then he got up and left. He may have been bummed out because I told him that I was never going to lend him money again. But it was not the last memory of my father I wanted.

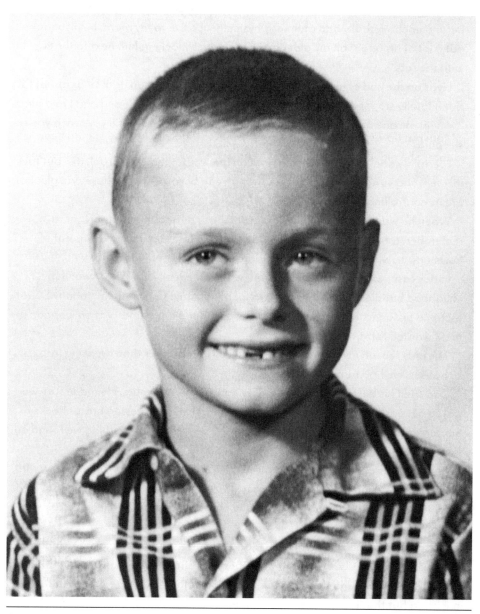
Bruce Landon.
(Photo courtesy Landon Family)

Jessie Florence May Landon was the glue that somehow kept our family together. A war bride who had met my father when he was stationed in London, England, she was a seamstress and made all my clothes until I was about 16.

Mom never learned how to drive. She never graduated from high school. But she could do the New York Times crossword puzzle, and she used to destroy us when the TV show "Jeopardy" first came on the air.

Mom put up with more misery from my father than any woman should have to endure. She did it only for my brother and myself, and because she had no money and nowhere to go. Finally, she could not stand it any longer.

With the pressure building, mom was becoming an alcoholic herself. Her drink of choice was rye and water. One night in a bar, she met Oliver Smith, who became her good friend and just a shoulder for mom to lean on. After hearing how badly she was being treated, he asked her to move in with him.

At first, my brother and I were furious seeing our mother move in with another man, but we also had seen first-hand the abuse she was suffering. After meeting with
Oliver and listening to him tell us how he was going to care for our mother, we accepted it.

It turned out to be the best thing that happened for my mother. She divorced my father and married Smitty, and they enjoyed some great years together before his death. Most importantly, he lived up to his promise to Terry and me. He treated her well, and he also provided Mom with enough money so she could provide for herself after his death.

Mom started suffering from dementia in her 70s and later dealt with Alzheimer's disease. It has always bothered me that I was not around to help my brother take care of her. But I was 350 miles away from home and once again - as he'd done when he was younger - Terry had to carry the brunt of the responsibilities.

Mom had to move from her really cute mobile home to an assisted living facility and then, as her health declined, to a nursing home. How she died was a tragedy. She was sitting in another patient's wheelchair and, as I found out, Alzheimer's patients can get volatile. The lady who owned the chair became very angry and dumped Mom on to the floor.

She broke her hip and never recovered. She died peacefully in the hospital. I am at least at peace, knowing my brother and I were with her when she passed.

I know for certain that my life would have taken a different turn, had it not been for my older brother Terry. He was the star quarterback on his high school football team, a pole vaulting champion, the best basketball player on the team and a very good hockey player. He excelled in all sports - unlike myself, a one-sport specialist who could only stop hockey pucks.

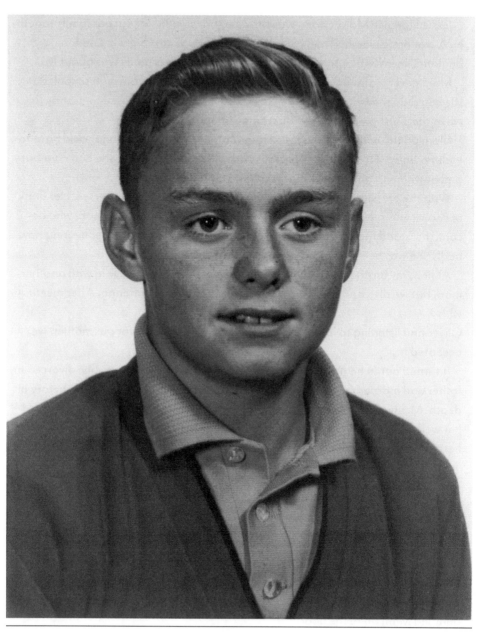

Bruce Landon.
(Photo courtesy Landon Family)

In fact, I became a goaltender because of him. Terry needed someone to shoot frozen tennis balls at, so I would put on my snow suit and he would stick me on the road between two rubber boots and take shots all day long. We never came in until Mom flipped the porch light on.

Terry eventually made the Junior A team at Niagara Falls, but he was not able to pursue his hockey career. He needed to return home to help out the family financially. Had he not chosen to do that, I would not have been able to pursue my own hockey dreams.

At age 19, Terry became a fireman, and unfortunately, most of his checks were turned over to the old man. He was never a great student, not because he was not smart enough, but because he was all consumed by sports - and I am sure the pressures at home did not help.

But he was certainly smart enough to realize he did not want to be on the back of a fire truck in sub-zero weather his entire life. Terry studied hard and went on to work himself up the proverbial ladder to become one of the youngest fire chiefs in the Province of Ontario.

Like most siblings, Terry and I had our battles. He would torment me at times and because I was not a good kid, I had to find a way to get even. One time I chased him around the house with a butcher knife - and I know that because of my temper, if I had caught him, I would have stabbed him.

I once threw a dart at him that stuck in his back. When he complained to our mother, she told him he should have gotten out of the way. Terry always thought Mom favored me more.

After our father lost the house and we moved to the apartment, Terry and I had to share the same bedroom. At the time, he was dating Shari Mills, the mayor's daughter and a beautiful cheerleader. I used to get steamed because he would come home late at night and yank me out of bed or turn on the lights, just to annoy me. So typically, one night I decided to get even.

Terry never wore a tee shirt or pajama top when he went to bed. I got out the tooth picks and put them in the holes of our cribbage board, put the board in his bed and covered it with his sheet. I also took the light bulb out so he could not turn on the lights.

At about 2 am., Terry came in. Just as I was hoping, he pulled back the covers and jumped in to bed. I am sure the people living five floors below us could hear him screaming from the pain of all the toothpicks stuck in his bare back. It drew blood, so my mission was accomplished.

Despite all of our brotherly practical jokes and arguments, some of which probably went too far, Terry never once hit me, and he always had my back when I would get into trouble, which I did way too often. It's a good thing he did.

Brother Terry Landon was a good hockey player.
(Photo courtesy Landon Family)

Marcia Landon with daughters Tammy and Tracey. (Photo courtesy Landon Family)

When I was 18 and returned home for the summer after Junior hockey season, I was able to get into one of the bars in the Village. It was a seedy place, so they didn't care that I was underage. I had become very good at arm wrestling and I would start bragging about how I had never been beaten.

One night, I was challenged by a great big bastard who had put away far too many Labatts. I took on the challenge and put him down very quickly, and he was fuming. He grabbed his beer bottle, broke it over the table and was getting ready to stick it to me.

But Terry jumped in, grabbed the guy by the arm and put an end to what could have become my first barroom brawl.

Terry had to deal with much too much growing up in those early years, and I know at times I did not make things easier for him. I know he is very proud of my accomplishments, but I don't know if he really understands how proud I am of him.

What I also know that not for his love and support, my life would have taken a nasty turn for the worse. If he never knew it before, I hope he does now.

3
THE EARLY YEARS

I have always believed that my work ethic and willingness to do whatever it takes to get the job done - lessons I learned early in life - were the primary reasons I had any kind of success in the later years.

We never had any money as kids, so there was no such thing as an allowance. If you wanted anything, you had to work for it. Not a lot of my summer jobs (and there were many) lasted long, but each one taught me a little something different, and these lessons would help me later.

At 16, I started flipping hamburgers at a place called Clarke's Drive-in. The spot also had a gas pump, so in between jobs on the grill, I would run out and fill someone's car up with gas and clean the windshields.

I had it timed perfectly where I could throw on a burger, then get to the car and get back without burning the place down. No one ever complained about the smell of gas on their food, either.

The burger/gas station gig also serves us a constant reminder to one of the most tragic events to have ever happened in my life. I had turned 18, returned home from my season in Peterboro and was back working at the diner again. A good friend of mine, John Dover, stopped in to say hello and asked if I wanted to jump on the back of his motorcycle and go over to Clayton, New York with him.

This was about 45 minutes from Kingston and the drinking age was 18. I was working, so I had to pass on the offer.

Another friend of mine, Keith Harvey, who was 17, asked if he could borrow my license because he was going to go with John. Like a stupid teenager, I gave it to him. It was the last time I saw either John or Keith alive.

On their way home that night, the motorcycle did not make a curve and crashed into a brick wall. The police identified one of the bodies as Bruce Landon because of my I.D., which was being carried by Keith. Two kids who knew me were following the motorcycle in their car; they stopped and told the cops that it was not me.

I received a strong lecture from the police and my parents, but no other punishment other than a memory that sometimes is still too vivid in my mind. I still ask myself, after all these years if they'd have still made that trip had I had not given Keith my license.

I also got fired from a couple of summer jobs, and for good reasons. As my mother would say, at times I was a rotten kid. I was only 15 when I went to work for a hard-nosed Portuguese man who used to put down Terrazzo flooring. I was just a grunt worker and had to haul the tiles from the truck.

One day, I walked in the front door with a big load of new tiles on my shoulder. I did not realize it, but a new layer of tiles had just been put down and they had not dried yet. I wiped out about ten feet of tiling and went sliding across the floor. He kicked me in the butt with a wet boot and he shoved me out the door, swearing like hell.

I think I now know the words for "(bleeping) idiot" in Portuguese.

One summer, my brother and I were desperate to find some summer work to make a couple of bucks. We took a weekend job at Sears, but it only lasted about three hours.

Our job was to move some mattresses from the top floor to the basement, but we had to use the stairs. We spent the first hour trying to figure out how we were going to do it, and the next two hours laughing like maniacs. My brother Terry stuck me in a mattress like a hot dog and pulled the sides up so I could slide down the stairs.

I made the first turn like an Olympic bobsledder, but then I lost my grip. The mattress sprang open, hurdling me down a couple flights of stairs. To this day, when my wife asks me to flip our mattress, I have flashbacks of a Sears manager walking me out the door.

4
MINOR HOCKEY AND THE JUNIOR YEARS

Our house was across the street from a small park, and that provided the beginning for me to become a goaltender. Older brother Terry needed a target, so he bundled me up in a snow suit and dragged me across the street. He would stick me between two rubber boots that acted as goal posts and start shooting frozen tennis balls at me.

This was our daily routine before school. After school, we would stay out until Mom would flick on the outside lights. Like most Canadian kids, we were out on the ponds all the time, no matter what the weather was like. Ball hockey was played all year long, even in the hot days of summer. It was hockey, hockey and more hockey all the time.

Every kid dreamed of being the next Gordie Howe or Jean Beliveau. All I wanted to be was the next Glenn Hall, my idol who played for Chicago.

When I was 8 years old and playing forward for our Church Athletic team, we had one game on a bitterly cold and windy morning at the outdoor rink - and our goaltender never showed up. I decided to put on these oversized green goalie pads, played my first game between the pipes and never looked back.

Having found my calling in hockey, I moved on to a team called the Hawks in the Minor Hockey Association and quickly established myself as one of the best goaltenders in the area. I hate to be pompous about it, but I made all-star teams in Peewee, Bantam and then Midget levels, and this was when my hockey career really evolved.

Hey, it's not bragging if it's true, right?

I was named Most Valuable Player of a Midget tournament held every year in

Trenton, Ontario. This is recognized as one of the best tournaments in Canada, and after the final game, a hockey scout for the Montreal Canadiens named Bill "Squeak" Reason came to the dressing room.

He offered me a chance to try out in the fall for the Peterborough Petes, a dominant Junior A team. "Squeak" gave me the option of also trying out for the Chatham Maroons Junior B team, which was in a very competitive league in Western Ontario. His advice was that he thought I would make the Junior B team, where I would play a lot and therefore have a chance to further develop.

So, in September at the age of 15, with about 20 bucks in my pocket, I jumped on a bus for the 400-mile ride from Kingston to Chatham. It was the start of a journey that would take me from my hometown for good.

After a nine-hour bus ride we arrived in Chatham, where I was met by the team trainer. He was taking me to my first Junior practice, where I would have one chance to show I was good enough to make the team.

Despite being dog-tired from the trip, I made a good impression and was told after practice that I had earned a spot on the club. I was driven to my billet's house, where I would live for the season with local people. I walked up the stairs and another player, Paul Grills, with whom I was to share a room, took one look at me and threw a tube of Clearasil at me.

He said, "You are full of pimples, you need this," which was not the nicest way to welcome a nervous kid who was living away from home for the first time. But Paul turned out to be a great guy, and to this day, one of the funniest guys I have ever met.

His mom was a nurse, so she was able to keep me stocked up on my acne cream.

The Western Ontario Junior B League was very physical and at some point, in every game, a fight or two would break out. The rivalries were intense and there were as many fights in the stands. We had a big Finnish kid, Seppo Ruuska, who was one of the toughest and meanest players in the league, and predictably, he was in the middle of it when a big brawl broke out at the end of one game in Strathroy.

Seppo was kicking the daylights out of their star player, when suddenly, the doors at the end of the rink opened and fans started running onto the ice. We started whacking away at these crazy nut jobs, and they were being chopped down like firewood when the police finally showed up.

We needed protection to get to the dressing room, and after two hours of waiting, we had a police escort out of town. That was life in the Junior Bs.

I had a good season in Chatham and by the next year, I was able to move up to the Peterborough Petes of the Ontario Junior A League. This was in the mid-1960s, when the league was regarded at the time as the number-one feeder system for the National Hockey League.

Roger Neilson gives his acceptance speech upon being inducted into the Hockey Hall of Fame in Toronto on Monday, Nov. 4, 2002. Neilson, 68, head coach of eight NHL teams was inducted in the builders category. (AP Photo/ Dave Sandford)

Our coach was the legendary Roger Neilson, who not only possessed a great hockey mind, but was a mentor - and for me, a father figure at a time in my life when I needed it most. Roger is famous for doing some crazy and bizarre things as a coach, and the rule book of the NHL, where he coached for eight different teams from 1977 to 2002, was rewritten a couple of times because of him.

I was part of one of those crazy episodes. It happened in Junior A but caused a ripple-effect all the way to the National Hockey League.

We were playing an exhibition game against the Toronto Marlies, a dominant team at that time in the Ontario Hockey League. A small skilled forward named Terry Caffery (who would cross paths with my life years later, during my contract negotiations in the WHA) was awarded a penalty shot against us.

Roger took me out of the nets for the shot. In my place, he put 6-foot-5 defenseman Ron Stackhouse, who was obviously not wearing goalie equipment. Roger instructed Stackhouse to charge out at Caffery just as he was crossing the blue line.

It worked to perfection. The big, lanky defenseman rushed out and as Caffery tried to go around him, Stackhouse just knocked the puck off his stick.

It happened again during a regular season game, and again, Neilson took me out of the goal and put Stackhouse between the pipes for the penalty shot.

Again, Stackhouse was able to make a play that prevented a goal being scored.

The National Hockey League took notice and a rule was changed, stating that a goaltender could not be replaced by a forward or a defenseman, only by another goaltender.

To win hockey games, Roger was not afraid to really think outside the box. The big powerhouse during my two years in the OHL was the Montreal Junior Canadiens. They were stacked with several top players, including Rejean Houle and Marc Tardiff, both of whom would go on to good NHL careers.

They would routinely beat us badly every time we played them. When their offense got cranked up, there was nothing we could do to stop them, with the exception of one game when we played them in our home rink.

We had taken a 2-1 lead, but the Canadiens were all over us and starting to take over when the game came to a halt. An egg had come flying down onto the ice, and the ice crew had to come out and clean it up.

The game restarted and after a while, we were still clinging to a 3-2 lead despite being badly outshot. Play once again was stopped as another egg was splattered onto the ice.

The Canadiens were getting frustrated as they lost their momentum, but this same scene played out a few more times during the game, and we hung on to win the game.

We found out a few weeks later that Roger, who was a teacher, had paid one of his young students to come to the game with a pocket full of eggs. Roger used to wear a fedora and he told the kid that every time he tapped the top of his hat, the kid was to throw one of the eggs and then move to a different part of the arena.

Roger made it very clear to all his players that you went to school and played hockey and no matter what time we got home from a road game, if you did not get to school on time the next day, you would be suspended. There was one exception, though.

One night, we had returned home from a long bus ride from Montreal and got back to our home rink around 3 am. Roger had a German shepherd named Jock who used to sit at his feet on the bus and go to all the games. On this particular morning as we were unpacking the bus, Jock disappeared.

It was about five degrees with a pretty good snowstorm, and Roger was going out of his mind because he could not find his dog. He told the entire team to spread out and start looking for Jock. After about two hours Roger called the players back in to the rink. He had found his dog.

When the bus doors had opened, Jock had gone into the arena and was curled up sleeping under Roger's desk. We had spent two hours freezing our butts off, but at least we were able to miss morning classes.

Roger Neilson's impact on me reflected how much he meant to so many kids, adult pros and hockey itself. In 2002, one year before he died at the too-young age of 69, he was inducted into the Hockey Hall of Fame - appropriately enough in the "builder" category.

During my second year in Peterborough, I needed to attend school only in the morning to get my high school diploma. Unlike most of the other kids, though, I had very little money, so I had to get a part-time job in the afternoon. I landed a job in a men's clothing store, which made no sense at all since many of the clothes I was still wearing were threads my mother had made for me.

My roommate was Ron Stackhouse, that big defenseman who had filled in at goal for the penalty shots, and a skilled player who went on to play for the Pittsburgh Penguins. As laid-back as they come, Ron also owned a bright brand new red Javelin, which turned out to be good for me.

Stacker did not have to go to school and on most mornings, he would throw me the keys to his car, lean over, put a Gordon Lightfoot record on the stereo and go back to sleep. He would still be there when I would return home from school at noon before going off to my clothing-store gig.

My second year in Peterborough was also my draft year, which meant if I had a good season, there was a chance some NHL team would select me in the June draft. This was 1968 and the draft was not a big event like it is today, where all the players, families and agents gather in the host city, waiting for your name to be called.

For us, it was a phone call - if you were fortunate enough to get selected. I'd had a great year and led the league in shutouts, and I got the call I was hoping for. I found out that I had been selected by the Los Angeles Kings.

It was, of course, a big deal for a teenager. What I didn't know at the time was how much this call would eventually change my personal and professional life.

5

FIRST PRO CAMP

My first professional camp with the Los Angeles Kings was held in the fall of 1969 in Barrie, Ontario, which is about two hours from my hometown of Kingston. Most pros never forget the experience of attending their first camp, and I was no exception. It was memorable - in more ways than one.

I had gone to camp unsigned and I got off to a great start. I realized after the first day of practice that I could handle it, so I was not nearly as nervous as I thought I'd be. My first big chance to play came in two preseason games against the Detroit Red Wings.

This is when I began to learn how fragile life in pro hockey could be. Some things can be controlled, but some cannot, as I found out in the second game when I suffered a concussion - the first of several I would endure over my career.

It came late in the second period after I had crouched down low to avoid being screened. That's when I took a Bobby Baun slap shot to the forehead, the force of which split my mask in half and knocked me backward into the net.

The trainers came out and helped me to my feet. I wanted to stay in the game, but they knew I was completely out of it when I skated to the wrong bench and puked my guts out. But this was the late 1960s, there was no concussion protocol in those days and I was back at practice the next day.

I can only wonder what would have happened without the mask. In one respect, I was lucky: Jacques Plante had pioneered the use of a mask in 1959, and plenty of goalies still refused to wear them into the 1960s. Andy Brown was the last player not to wear one, and his World Hockey Association career ended almost at the same time as mine.

My career began at about the time masks were becoming universally accepted. Thank God for that, but even with the masks, serious injuries and concussions were occupational hazards for goaltenders.

There was no doubt I was the best goalie in camp, and management kept saying it in the local newspapers. Larry Regan, the Kings general manager, and chief scout George Maguire started pressuring me to sign a contract.

I had no agent, but I was ready to stand up to them because of my play. I figured that since they kept telling everyone how good I was, maybe I had some leverage.

The first offer they made was me was for $15,000 if I made the Los Angeles Kings and $8,000 if I was sent to the AHL. I was also offered a signing bonus of $2.000. I was only 19 at the time and had about 50 bucks in my jeans, so you would think I'd have jumped at the offer.

But I could be a stubborn pain in the neck, even back when I was 19. Maybe it was back in that first camp that I really started believing you had to have the courage of your convictions. So, I thought if I held out a bit longer, they would up the ante, but at the same time, I was scared to death that they would send me packing.

After a double session on the ice, where the shooters could not get a puck past me, Maguire paid a visit to my hotel room. It was the first time I was threatened by management, though not the last.

He said I was attacking him personally by not signing, because he had gone out on a limb by recommending the Kings draft me. I was given two options: either sign the new contract they were going to offer me, or as he put it, "get the (hell) out of Dodge."

I would soon get my first taste of how NHL management will try to fill you with a bunch of nonsense and manipulate the situation. The new offer delivered by Regan upped the NHL salary to $16,000 and the AHL contract to $8,500, and they also agreed to bump my signing bonus to $3,000.

I had won the battle, or so I thought because they had, in fact, made small increases from the original offer. I was still hesitating until they told me it was the very same money they had given Dale Hoganson, who was their first draft pick that year. If it was good enough for a first-round pick, the thinking went, it was good enough for me.

Word got around camp that I had signed and the next day after practice, I was having a beer with Hoagie and a couple of other players. He congratulated me on my new contract and said he was happy they had given me the same signing bonus of $10,000 that he'd received. I had been given the royal shaft, but I learned a valuable lesson that I carried with me the rest of my life: never trust anyone when it comes to your money.

We only had four rookies at camp that first year. There was Hoganson,

Butch Goring, defenseman Greg Boddy and me. Every afternoon after practice, the veteran guys like Bill "Cowboy" Flett, Dave Amadio, Dale Rolfe and others would play poker at the hotel. Then one day, shortly after I had signed, they asked me if I wanted to play.

I think they wanted to get a piece of my signing bonus and thought since I was a rookie, it would be easy money for them. But I I'd been playing poker since I was about 14 years old, so I knew how to play.

I also knew that I only had 50 bucks. But I got lucky and turned that into almost a $200 profit.

The next morning in practice, every shot taken was at my head. I was clueless as to what was going on until Flett skated up to me and said, "You were lucky at cards yesterday, but there's another game today. Make sure you are there."

I made sure I showed up and I also folded a few times when I knew I had a winning hand. The vets got some of their money back and I survived the rest of camp.

On the last day of camp, Kings management - led by Coach Hal Laycoe, Regan and Maguire - called me into their temporary office at the hotel. I was told, right to my face, that I was the best goalie the entire camp and that I had made the National Hockey League. I was given orders to get back to Kingston for a couple of days of rest then meet the team in Toronto to fly out to the West Coast, where we would open up the season.

I called my brother and my parents, and I was crying like a newborn. I had realized a dream that I had worked so hard and sacrificed so much to earn. I was a 19-year-old rookie - and I had made the Los Angeles Kings.

Hell, I was even going to take my first ride on an airplane.

My family decided to throw a small party with a few of my friends to celebrate when I got back to Kingston. Our partying gave me the chance to tell stories about my first pro camp experiences, embellishing most of it them - until 2 a.m., when I received a phone call that would dramatically change my career and my personal life.

While I was preparing for the NHL career I'd been promised, Kings management had held a long meeting after camp had broken and decided that even though I deserved to be playing alongside Gerry Desjardins in Los Angeles, I would benefit by going to their farm team in Springfield. They broke the news to me with that early morning phone call, I was devastated.

If not for the advice of my brother. I'd have quit hockey on the spot. I could not believe that with one frigging phone call, I was not going to sunny California, but to a city I had never heard of, and had no idea where it was.

I would not be making my first plane trip after all. Instead, I would be getting on a Greyhound bus out of Kingston and heading for Springfield, Massachusetts.

The rest, as they say, is history.

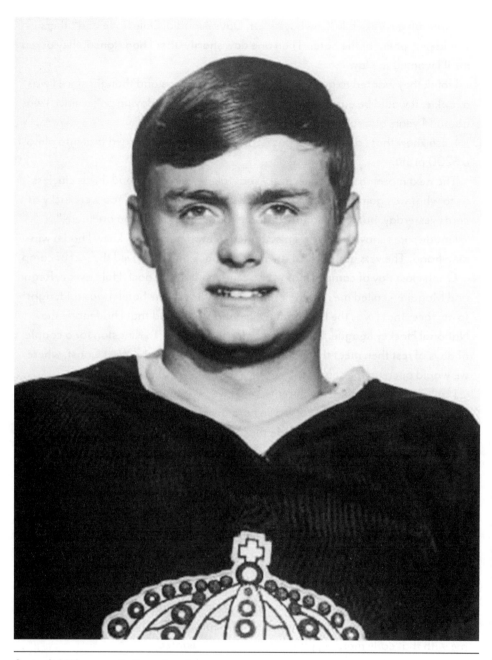

Springfield Kings goalie Bruce Landon.
(From the Springfield Kings Hockey Magazine for the 1969-70 Season).

6

THE SPRINGFIELD KINGS

Kingston to Springfield is an easy, nearly six-hour ride by car, but on a ratty old bus that stopped at every one-horse town along the way, it took me about 12 hours to finally pull in to the Peter Pan Bus Terminal in downtown Springfield. I find it somewhat ironic now that Peter Picknelly Jr., the son of the man who owned the bus company that gave me my first taste of Springfield, would many years later become one of my business partners.

I grabbed a Yellow Taxi for what should have been a quick ride to our training camp headquarters at the Agawam Motor Lodge. The place was torn down in the decade of the 2010s. Based on what I saw in 1969, it should have been bulldozed back then.

Exhausted, I finally got to my room around 3 am in the morning, not long before I had to be up early for my first practice with the Springfield Kings. I could not find a light for the room, so instead, I switched on the bathroom light. I can still picture it like it was yesterday.

About ten cockroaches found hiding places from the light. For my first night in Springfield, I slept with my clothes on. The entire experience was a culture shock for a rookie like myself who had played Junior hockey in a beautiful arena in Canada.

There was more to come. When I showed up for the first day at the Eastern States Coliseum in West Springfield, I was in total shock. I could not believe that a pro team would play in this old barn.

The ice surface looked no bigger than one of the backyard rinks I'd played on as a kid. There were wooden seats and wooden floors, and the place was saturated with an old damp cigarette smell. And I could not believe the small and cramped layout of the dressing room.

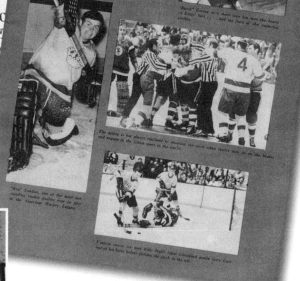

Top Left: "Springfield Kings Directorate." [From the Springfield Kings Hockey Magazine for the 1969-70 Season].

Center: Cover of the Springfield Kings Hockey Magazine for the 1969-70 Season.

Left: Jimmy Anderson on December 15, 1969. (Photo by Art MacGannell, Springfield Union/Republican file photo).

Bruce Landon makes a save in his professional debut with the Springfield Kings with Noel Price looking on, 1969. (Photo by Stephen N. Lemanis, The Republican).

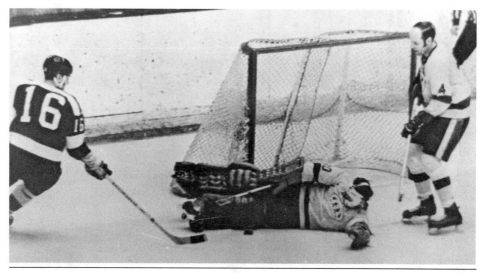

Another dramatic save by Bruce Landon as a Springfield Kings goaltender, 1969. (Photo from Pictures Inc., copy by George Loons).

As a rookie, I was given a seat right next to the shower and the toilet, which was all in the same cramped space. There were only two shower heads and the floor was made of wooden pallets, so you could look down and see all the crud on the bottom. The toilet door never shut all the way, so if you went in to take a dump, the guys in the shower could watch you wipe your ass. Even for minor league standards in 1969, it was pretty disgusting.

Despite the horrible conditions, trainer Peter Demers and Andy Burgess, the equipment man, did their best to keep the room as clean as possible. That much was a plus, at least.

Most athletes can vividly recall their first pro game. I was no exception. I got the nod to start against the Baltimore Clippers, posted a 6-0 shutout and was named the first star of the game. With that came a gift certificate to Yale & Genton a men's clothing store and the perfect gift for a newcomer to town, since I certainly needed some new threads.

Thanks to Jim Denver, the long-time supervisor of off-ice officials, I was not the least bit nervous for my pro debut. Just before going out on the ice for the start of the game, Jim sat me down and told me a pretty raunchy joke that cracked me up. I think I was still chuckling under my mask when the national anthem was being played.

Jim passed away many years ago but the Denver family, especially his son Jay and granddaughter Kate, have become lifelong friends.

I still have the newspaper article from the game written by Sam Pompei, a veteran hockey writer for the Springfield Newspapers. In it, Larry Regan - the Los Angeles Kings general manager who had sentenced to me to Springfield rather than LA - was quoted as saying, "We said all along he was the best goalie in Canada, which is why we drafted him."

It would have been nice if he'd remembered that a week earlier, when he was giving me the shaft with my contract.

I don't hold many records, but I am proud of the fact that I believe that, to this day, I am the only rookie goalie in Springfield hockey history to have recorded a shutout in his first professional game. I went on to win my first five games and the accolades were coming from everywhere. The more stories I read about how great I was, the more my head swelled.

The veteran guys on the team made sure that my cockiness did not last long, so they decided it was time for my rookie initiation. I had stayed out after practice for a little extra work and I had just finished the last shooting drill, when I looked up and saw five of the older guys with white towels wrapped around their heads coming toward me. I had no clue what the hell was going on until I heard them start singing the Gillette razor song from the commercials. That told me something was about to happen. It did. They tackled me and they carried me off the ice to the dressing room, removed my equipment stripped me naked. They had a towel wrapped around my eyes, so I could not see what was going on and I could not identify the ringleader. In the middle of the dressing room was an old rickety table that the trainers would leave towels on for the guys going into the shower. When I was thrown on my back onto the table, I could hear the legs start creaking under my weight.

It gets painful even now to talk about what happened next.

All I could feel was them tying a skate lace around my penis, and I heard them talking how they were going to tie the other end to a pipe above the table. They then decided to shave my entire chest and pubic hair.

Every time I squirmed to try and get free, someone would give the skate lace a little tug. I could feel the skin on my male member being scraped away. I thought it was over, until the guy leading the group of barbers decided to shave off one of my eyebrows and some of the hair on my head.

This extra punishment came because I had become just a little too cocky. Players would serve jail time today if they tried this kind of stunt.

The timing of my rookie initiation could not have been worse. A few days prior to the hazing, I had suffered a cut in practice and had to see our team doctor for stitches to my chin. Dr. Coons had a beautiful young assistant working for him, and I really wanted to ask her out on a date. However, with a half-shaven head and only one eyebrow, it would have to wait.

A couple of weeks later when the hair had grown in - and over a couple of bottles of courage - I made the call. Little did I know at the time that this call would introduce me to Marcia Lee Oliver, who would become my future wife.

No, I am not sure when she found out about the pubic hair. In case you're wondering.

Marcia and I hit it off from the first time we went out. Years later, I found out that her parents had been really, really displeased that she was dating a hockey player. They were concerned I would be taking her off to some remote Canadian city and they would never see her again.

Marcia actually told her parents she only wanted to go out on one date with me. I must have been a hell of a first date, because as of this writing, we see our 50-year golden anniversary of marriage coming into view.

After only dating Marcia for a few months, I asked her father if I could marry her. I will never forget what he said. He knocked on his head three times and said, "Sure you can, but you must have rocks in your head."

Now, when I visit the Veterans Cemetery, which I do a couple of times a month, I say my prayers and then I always knock three times on his headstone. Somehow, I sense that he hears it and is happy his daughter and I are happy in our senior years - and that she is not living in the woods in Canada.

Over my long career, first as a player and later in management, I could never figure out the rationale behind some of the decisions that were made. Although my first year as a pro was a success, I am still miffed at what happened that year during the playoffs.

I had been the number one goaltender all year and a goalie named Bob Sneddon was my backup. Jimmy Anderson, a legendary figure as a player for the Springfield Indians (which had been an independent team before the 1967 NHL expansion led to Los Angeles' purchase of the franchise) had taken over as coach after Johnny Wilson was promoted to the LA Kings.

We opened the playoffs against the Hershey Bears, and I was given the start. With myself and Sneddon splitting the goaltending, we beat the Bears in seven games.

I was not great. But then, we played a "sudden death" game against the powerful Montreal Voyageurs, in Montreal, to see who would advance to the finals against the Buffalo Bisons. The Bisons were playing their last AHL season before Buffalo joined the NHL as an expansion team (the Sabres) that fall.

Anderson selected me to play the sudden-death game. Facing a Canadiens farm team in Montreal was the tallest of orders, but we beat them 3-2 in what may have been my own best game of the year. It didn't matter to Anderson. In the finals against Buffalo, he went with Sneddon. We were swept in four straight games. I did not see one minute of playing time.

To this day, I have no idea what was going through Anderson's mind. I tried to figure out if I had done something to set him off. There was no logical reason as to why I did not get a chance to play in the finals.

My one regret is that I never asked him about this decision. Jimmy passed away a few years ago, so I will never know. But it was not the first time I would shake my head at some of things coaches do, and it wouldn't be the last.

7

SECOND PRO CAMP

My second pro camp was a train wreck. There's no other way to put it.

Camp was held in beautiful Victoria, British Columbia and, based on the success of my rookie year, Los Angeles Kings management had made it very clear they expected me to take over a spot on the NHL roster. On the first day of camp, I smashed my thumb so badly on my catching hand that I should have been out for a couple of weeks.

But I could not afford to take any time off, because there was a new young goalie in town. Billy Smith had been drafted 59th overall, and he was gunning for my job.

I had the trainer wrap my thumb, stuff my catching glove with thick cotton and tape it all up. The glove weighed about thirty pounds. I could not catch the puck - all I could do was bat it down, if I was lucky enough to even be able to lift it.

Fortunately for me, Smitty was not having a good camp either. We roomed together and one day he broke down so much that he was almost in tears. He was struggling so much that he thought they were going to send him back to his hometown in Perth, Ontario.

Training camp back then was always an interesting time. You have the veteran guys who knew pretty much they had a spot locked up. There were always a couple of guys who were never going to make it. And then there were the "tweeners," - bubble guys who had been handed the bullshit by management that if they have a great camp, there would be a spot open for them.

I heard the same speech every year I played. It always went something like this, "I don't care if you are a veteran guy, a first-round pick or the last guy drafted. We are going with the best players and the ones that deserve to be on the team."

It never happened that way. After about two days of camp, you could sense where you fit in with their plans. Sometimes it was just by which seat you were assigned in the dressing room, and who else was in that room.

You really got the message if you were not given a chance to play in a preseason game. You knew you were doomed to be sent down when they took your picture on media day in black and white, rather than in color like some of the guys.

The highlight in camp for me, since I was playing so poorly, was getting a chance to meet some of the guys who were real characters in the game. One of them was the unpredictable Eddie Shack, who had gained a reputation as being one of the game's most colorful and craziest players during his time in Toronto and Boston. Some of the stories about Shack are legendary, but since I've only heard about them, I am not sure they are true. However, based on my own first-hand experience with him, they're all easy to believe.

There was concern in 1970 that Shack was going to be a no-show, because he wanted a new contract and the Kings had not given him one. They also made it very clear to him that he would be given a hefty fine for each day he missed.

On the first day of camp, we were to begin at 6 a.m. with outdoor exercises led by a military guy the Kings had brought in. Eddie was not there. We were just getting ready to start when we heard the noise of a helicopter landing near us - after which Eddie jumped out dressed in a sweat suit and sneakers and started doing push-ups.

The training camp hotel was the first-class Empress Hotel, a far cry from the Agawam Motor Lodge. John Wayne used to park his yacht right across the street from the Empress. One day early in camp, the guys were going to go golfing after practice and I was invited to go along.

I had just gotten off the elevator with my golf bag over my shoulder when I saw a bunch of the players huddling in the middle of the lobby. They were cracking up as they watched Shack with a pitching wedge in his hand, trying to lob golf balls over a very expensive chandelier.

Due to the injury I had suffered on my left (catching hand) thumb and the fact I could not stop a beach ball throughout most of camp, I expected the news that I would be returning to Springfield. I was disappointed, naturally, because I thought maybe the Kings were losing interest in me. But they promised that if I got healthy and got off to a good start, I would get my chance to be called up.

They did give me that offer and I believe they meant it, but unfortunately, it never worked out. I played my first three seasons in Springfield, and later spent five years with the World Hockey Association's New England Whalers - with a brief detour in Providence and a return to the Springfield thrown in - but I never got to play in a NHL regular season game for the Los Angeles Kings.

8
RETURN TO SPRINGFIELD

Returning to Springfield for my second pro year was not what I wanted from a hockey standpoint, but for personal reasons, I was happy. My relationship with Marcia had blossomed to where it was time to start making plans for the future.

Cy and Lena Oliver, my future in-laws, asked me to move into their home in West Springfield. Marcia and I were now engaged, and they thought it would enable us to save some money. The Oliver's owned a very nice home, but it only had two bedrooms and there was no way Marcia and I would be sharing one of them. So, they set up a nice bed for me at the end of their spacious living room.

Lena would cook my pregame steaks for me, and I settled in as part of the Oliver family.

I had made them a promise that after we were married, we would not move back to Canada. But that first summer of marriage was probably the closest I have ever come to getting divorced, when I decided we should spend the summer in my hometown in Kingston.

Marcia did not appreciate me going out and drinking with my buddies more than I should have been. I think the final blow came when she went downstairs one morning and found one of my friends passed out on top of the stereo cabinet.

Having fully recovered from my training camp injury, I was given the starting role in Springfield, and Billy Smith was to be my backup. I got off to a great start and the call I had been waiting for came from the Kings, as they had promised. I was being recalled to the NHL and would get my first start in Boston.

To say I was pumped up would be a gross understatement. The Kings wanted me to play on Friday night in Springfield against Hershey, then go to Boston to play against the Bruins the next day.

New York Islander goaltender, Billy Smith makes a glove save against the New York Rangers, April 9, 1984. (Republican file photo).

It was not to be.

Halfway through the first game, Hershey winger Michel Harvey stormed in off the wing and cut in front of the net. I sprawled out to make the save and in doing so, I heard my shoulder pop. I was carried off to the dressing room where our trainer and the team doctor put the shoulder back in place.

So much for my NHL debut. I was on the shelf for about three weeks and even though I still had pain, I convinced our coach, Johnny Wilson, that I was ready to play again. Smitty was struggling, and there was no way I could let him take over the number-one duties.

I started playing well and the Kings called and again wanted me to make my NHL debut. But this is where things really get fouled up: I was becoming the local version of Ripley's Believe it or Not.

By sheer coincidence, we were again scheduled to play Hershey. The Kings wanted me to get that game under my belt before being recalled. It was the same player, Michel Harvey who - at about the same time in the game - cut in off the wing.

Again, I sprawled to make a save but sure enough, I dislocated my shoulder. This time it was worse: my season was over. Billy Smith went on to become the number-1 goaltender, and he was outstanding in leading the Springfield Kings to a Calder Cup.

As Billy was beginning a career that would lead him to four Stanley Cups with the New York Islanders, a well-deserved place in the Hockey Hall of Fame and the answer to a trivia question ("Who, in 1979, became the first NHL goaltender credited with scoring a goal), I watched from the stands and wondered if my short career was over for good. The injuries were starting to take their toll on my body.

I was always happy for Billy's success. Several years after our time in Springfield, we crossed paths, I kidded him that if I had never been injured, he would have never become one of the best goalies in the history of the NHL.

The injury came when I was still young at 21. My hockey career was not over yet. The Kings flew me out to California for major shoulder surgery, which required me having a pin inserted to keep my shoulder in place. It is still there to this day, a gentle but poignant reminder that sometimes fate gets in the way, and things don't always play out the way you hope.

Bruce and Marcia Landon's wedding Photo. (Photo courtesy Landon Family).

9
MARCIA LANDON, MY FAVORITE FAN

There's a famous saying, one I have used more than once, that says, "behind every successful man is a strong woman." I have been blessed with a woman who has not been behind me through a pretty incredible journey, but right by my side.

Marcia and I were married at the very young age of 21, and at this writing, she has been my soul mate for 48 years. Although she hitched her marital wagon to a hockey guy, she never really understood the game too much and never really cared to learn. But that did not mean she didn't support me in my chosen career.

During my playing days, she never once saw me make a save, or let a goal in. As soon as the puck crossed the red line, she would look the other way and wait to hear the crowd's reaction before turning around.

Since I was certainly injury-prone with a torn thumb, knee, shoulder, various stitches and concussions, I think she was just afraid I would get hurt again. She also knew I let every goal bother me and she would feel my pain, especially if I'd let a soft one get by me.

Most athletes will tell you they try not to take the game home with them, but I say that's ridiculous. It's with you 24 hours a day. You just try to hide it the best you can.

I not only took the game home with me, there were a couple of times when my poor wife suffered the consequences. One of those unfortunate episodes came after I'd just played a home game for the Whalers and, to be blunt, I'd been horrible.

It was one of those games where I could not have stopped a balloon had it floated down from the nosebleed seats. I allowed eight goals and that cost us the game. A five-year old peewee probably could have stopped four of them.

Above: Landon Wedding Photo: Bruce and Marcia Landon [center]; Bruce's parents, Norm and Jess Landon [L]; and Marcia's parents, Cy and Lena Oliver [R]. (Photo courtesy Landon Family).

When I did manage to get my body in front of one, the fans gave me the mock cheer. I have no idea why coach Harry Neale did not pull me from the game. I think he was either trying to send a message to the team or just mess with my head.

When the game was over, even my teammates were a bit cold to me, which was unusual. Marcia was waiting for me in the wives' room, and I came out of the dressing room to a sound of silence. Not one word was said.

We made the half hour ride home to my house in West Springfield and Marcia did not speak to me. She went to bed and as was customary for me, I had a shot of Scotch to try to settle myself down. I could never sleep for hours after a game I played - no matter how well or badly I'd played - and on this night, I finally went to bed.

To make it worse, I had a terrible dream that I was climbing a mountain and just as I got to the top, I started to fall. As I did, I kicked my legs out, my arms were flailing and that woke me up.

Marcia rolled over and said, "Don't tell me you finally stopped one."

*Bruce Landon with his daughters Tracey and Tammy.
(Photo courtesy Landon Family).*

We had a similar scene on another night after returning home from a game. Marcia went to bed. I poured a Scotch. I had more than one, in fact.

Again, the dream came but this time, there was a big brawl on the ice and I was in a dandy fight with some other player. I threw a ferocious overhand right that hit my sleeping wife on the ear.

She woke up screaming and in tears, not knowing what the hell had just happened. All I was thinking was that I was glad she was not laying on her back as I could have done some serious dental damage. Who says you don't take the game home with you?

Marcia has been supportive throughout - not only during my playing days, but also when I went into management and later ownership. She only wanted what made me happy and never tried to discourage me in any way. She didn't think I was completely nuts when I wanted to buy the Orange Julius franchises that were for sale in the Western Massachusetts area. Thank God a smart banker talked me out of that one.

Nor did she ever asked why, when former Whaler teammate Brad Selwood and

[L-R] Marcia and Bruce Landon, and Lena Oliver, Marcia's mother, at the Mass Mutual Center, Oct. 1, 2005. (Photo by Jessica Hill, The Republican).

I were going to buy a bar in Enfield, Connecticut and name it the 3/30 club in recognition of our uniform numbers. That deal fell through when Selwood and I realized it was probably a bad decision we'd made over too many beers.

When I decided to retire as a player and take a management job with the Springfield Indians, she supported the decision and was probably relieved she did not have to watch me endure any more injuries. She was in favor of us buying the worm farm, too. That's actually the one time I wish she had not backed this stupid move on my part.

When I called her up and told her I was going to become an investor in a new hockey franchise I was trying to buy, she never once asked where I was going to get the money. She trusted my instincts and judgment, and knew I would do the right thing for my family.

Marcia has been there through all the good times and we have had our share. She has also been right there to help me get through the bad times and has given me the shoulder to lean on, far more than she should have had to do. Most of all, she has been a terrific mother to my wonderful kids, Tracey and Tammy and a doting, devoted "Mema" to Peter and Anna, our two beautiful grandchildren.

Who knew that when I was just a cocky rookie goaltender in 1969 that a couple of stitches in the chin would lead me to meeting the woman who would become my number one fan?

10
FAMOUS COLISEUM BRAWL

The 1970-71 season was a Calder Cup championship year for Springfield, and a difficult, injury-riddled personal season for me, but it was memorable for another, more ugly reason, too.

I almost got kicked out of the country for my part in a famous brawl at the Eastern States Coliseum.

At that time, both teams shared the same penalty box, which was located right next to the Kings' three-tiered bench. The backup goaltender each night was assigned the seat on the top level.

We were playing the Rochester Americans and our player, Dunc Rousseau, had squared off against the Amerks' Red Armstrong in one hell of a fight. They were both sent to the penalty box and, as was customary, a West Springfield police officer took a seat between them. It took all of thirty seconds before words were exchanged, at which point the cop was pushed out of the way and punches started to fly.

It was then that the cop, in my opinion, made a mistake of grabbing Rousseau by the arms. Armstrong let loose and started pummeling Dunc, who could not do anything to protect himself.

Pete Demers, our trainer who weighed in at about 140 pounds, was closest to the penalty box. He jumped in to try freeing the cop's arm so Rousseau could defend himself. That was when all hell broke loose.

As soon as Pete touched the cop, every police officer in the building swarmed in to the area and started pulling Demers out of the bench. I was in full goalie gear and sitting on the bench, but Peter was my roommate, so I had to help out.

Springfield Kings players drinking champagne out of the Calder Cup after winning the 1971 AHL championship. (Photo by Stephen N. Lemanis, The Republican).

I jumped into the penalty box to get Demers free of the officer's grip. That was a mistake; I was soon dragged down the hall by two police officers and pinned against the wall. This all happened shortly after I had returned from my first shoulder injury. I asked the cop to let go of me because my shoulder was still sore and when he did, I popped him a good one. In the ensuing fracas, his uniform shirt also got torn pretty badly.

I was finally escorted to the dressing room, but no sooner had I been seated when coach, Johnny Wilson, came in to tell me the cops were arresting me, and they would be taking me to the police station. I was allowed to shower, but when I got dressed and walked out of the dressing room, I was surrounded by about ten police officers. I was told to get in the middle of them and they shuffled me off to the police car.

I was charged with assaulting a police officer and disturbing the peace. This made front page news the next day, not only in the Springfield papers, but in my hometown newspaper in Canada. I can just picture my mom saying, "I always said he was a rotten kid."

At this time, I was going through the process of applying for my green card. I was getting married in the off-season and we wanted to make our home in West Springfield. With a criminal record, there was no way I would be allowed to live in the United States.

The Kings hired George Leary, a local attorney who, prophetically, would buy the team years later and hire me to work for him. George was able to keep getting the hearings about my case postponed, and I was allowed to keep playing, but thoughts of being deported constantly weighed on my mind.

But Leary had a plan. He wanted us to get in front of a judge who he knew was a hockey fan.

My day in court finally arrived. Able to convince the judge that I was a good guy, George made the case that any kind of conviction or record would not only end my career but would also mean I would never get to live in West Springfield.

The judge decided to dismiss all charges. My only penalty was that I had to pay for a new shirt for the cop who had had his shirt ripped during our fight.

I thought that would be my only penalty, but the big blow came a few days later, when American Hockey League President Jack Butterfield fined me $500 for bad representation of the league. I was only making $9,000 at the time. I never paid the fine, and I have no idea whether the Kings or George picked up the tab.

George Leary has been a part of my life in many important ways. He not only literally bailed me out of a possible jail term, he threw me a life preserver more than once during my career.

Fast-forward many years later after this incident: long after I had retired as a player, the story of the infamous brawl surfaced again. I was in a local barbershop

Springfield Sunday Republican

SPRINGFIELD, MASS., NOVEMBER 8, 1970

200 Hockey Fans Riot, 3 Arrested

Kings' Trainer, Goalie Booked

By GENE McCORMICK
Republican Sports Writer

Bedlam broke loose Saturday night at the Eastern States Coliseum in West Springfield during the Rochester - Springfield American Hockey League game, resulting in three arrests. Involved in a chain reaction of fights were members of both teams, two linesmen, some 200 fans from a crowd of 5599 and nearly 20 West Springfield policemen.

Arrested as result of the brawl were Bruce (Boo) Landon, Springfield's spare goaltender; Peter Demers, trainer for the Springfield club; and Sydney M. Duck, a spectator at the game.

Landon, 21, of Kingston, Ont., is charged with breach of the peace and two counts of assault on a police officer.

Demers, 21, of Coach Lite Apartments, Agawam, is charged with breach of the peace and assault on a police officer.

Duck, 24, of 98 Rockland St., Springfield, is charged with breach of the peace. He was released in $25 bail.

Landon and Demers were released in their own recognizance. All three will appear in court Monday for arraignment, police said.

The riot broke out on the ice between Norm Armstrong, the fiery redheaded captain of the Rochester team, and Springfield's Dunc Rousseau. Within minutes the fighting carried into the penalty bench area, out into the front lobby and finally spilled into the parking area in front of the Coliseum.

It took police and officials from both teams some 20

See HOCKEY
Page 49

The Western Mass. Schoolboy Soccer Tournament at Springfield College Saturday was marred by an unruly disturbance that the Chicopee - Ludlow semifinal game never did finish. At left, Bogan ejects a Ludlow player from game. At right, a fan kicks the official to start a disturbance which forced the game to be stopped.

Fans Blow Their Cool To Ruin Soccer Game

By MIKE BOGEN
Republican Sports Writer

High school soccer fans blew their cool at the Western Mass. Tournament Saturday at Springfield College.

They streamed onto the field, pushed officials and players and caused such a disturbance that the Chicopee - Ludlow semifinal game never did finish. The fans came onto the field following the ejection of Ludlow player Dennis Duarte by referee Paul Bogan.

Chicopee was declared the winner when the game was called with seven and one-half minutes left. The defending state champions were leading, 3-1, and the final score was listed as such.

Northampton nipped West Springfield, 2-1, in a semifinal game later in the day, when things had cooled. The Chicopee and 'Hamp will play for the Western Mass. Class L (large school) championship Wednesday at Springfield College.

Duarte, while arguing with the official, pushed him and was ejected. Another Ludlow player also bumped Bogan. Both benches and the stands emptied and a ten-minute melee ensued.

The first sign of the impending disturbance came at the end of the second period when, following a Chicopee goal, a spectator ran onto the field to argue with the referee. The man was escorted from the field but officials in the event of trouble. There were no fights

See CHICOPEE
Page 49

Rattling Resumes In San Francisco

SAN FRANCISCO (AP) — San Francisco's rickety, bell-banging cable cars resume operations today after a 2½-day absence.

Thirty operators walked off the job Thursday night in a rhubarb that developed with police after one of the cable cars and a truck collided.

Leakage Perils Hartford

ROCKY HILL, Conn. (AP) — A barge tied up at a Texaco Oil Co. facility here spilled thousands of gallons of gasoline onto the Connecticut River here Saturday.

A rising tide spread the volatile slick toward Hartford suburbs to the north.

At one point in Glastonbury, across the river from here, a layer of gasoline five feet deep was reported near the shore. Police went from house to house nearby, warning residents not to use gas stoves and to be careful about electrical equipment that might spark.

Heavy gasoline fumes could be smelled here and in Glastonbury. Officials were placed on alert in Hartford, about five miles to the south.

Officials also refused to allow photographers near the river, fearing their flash

See LEAKAGE
Page 2

$200 Graffiti Won by Prof.

Richard L. Weaver, 26-year-old speech professor at the University of Massachusetts, is the winner of the Republican-Union Go With Graffiti Contest.

The $200 grand prize goes to a man used to addressing the public. Weaver is a professor of speech.

Weaver's prize - winning entry was "Persuasion Is The Art of Moving Apathy In Your Direction," published in The Union Sept. 23.

Because of the large number of excellent graffiti entered, the task of choosing the best single entry was exceedingly difficult for the graffiti editor.

But there was a secondary consideration in making Weaver's excellent entry the ultimate choice in the two - month contest.

He submitted 10 other entries, all of them of merit. Weaver, 26, was born in Hanover, N.H., but later moved to Michigan and was graduated from the University of Michigan where he met his wife, Andrea. They were married while he was enrolled in a

See PROFESSOR
Page 10

Richard L. Weaver, 26-year-old speech professor at the University of Massachusetts and grand prize winner in the Republican-Union Go With Graffiti contest, holds some entries Saturday which failed to make the contest deadline.

Freight Train Takes Boys to Church

Two Springfield boys made an unscheduled train trip to Hartford Saturday, on an open flat car.

Joseph Vermette, 14, of 100 Union St. and his 11-year-old brother, John, were playing on a railroad car near Columbus Avenue when the train started, with the boys clinging on for dear life.

The train started in pick

up speed, so we found the safest spot we could, which was under a trailer truck, on the flat car," Joseph said. "I was scared to death. I had never been on a train like that before."

Roger Crosier of 104 West St., Chicopee, who had been playing with the Vermette boys, was not on the train, when it started.

"When the train started moving I tried to run along with it, but then it started moving too fast," he said. "I went to tell their mother."

Mrs. Helen Vermette, the boys' mother, called the Penn Central Railroad. A railroad official said they would try to get the boys off in Hartford, the train's first stop.

Mrs. Vermette also notified the Springfield police.

But the half - hour ride, huddled underneath the trailer truck, ended before a welcoming committee could be arranged for them at the Hartford station.

According to Joseph, they got off the train and started walking.

"We walked to Windsor,

about five and a half miles, when I thought of going to a church for help" Joseph said.

They knocked on the front door of St. Gabriel's Church in Windsor where Fr. Robert Delaney, listened to their story and took them in. Fr. Delaney described

See FREIGHT TRAIN
Page 32

Good Morning!

- Lady Bird's White House Diary 22
- The Day They Laughed at Lenin 30
- Memories of Charlie Root 50
- Stan Hunt's Corner 57

TODAY'S INDEX

Section 1
Chicopee 32
City News 14, 18, 28
Suburban 23, 32

Section 2
Amusements 38-39
Art 40
Bishop Sheen 37
Books 40
Camera 43
City News 35, 34
Confident Living 35
Crossword Puzzle 44
Editorial 46
Feeder Scraps 44

Music 41
Travel 42-43

Section 3
Financial 59-65
Sports 49-58

Section 4
Contract Bridge 77
Deaths 78
Gardens 79, 80
Home Improvements ... 75-77
Television 73-77
Women's News 66-74

Section 5
Classified ads 81-96

The Weather

Sunny Cooler Today, Milder Monday

getting my hair cut, when Ralphie the barber and I started talking hockey and he brought up the Coliseum fight.

He had been at the game, and according to Ralphie, he had the best seat in the house to watch it all. I told him about me punching the officer in the hallway. I had just finished the story, when a man a couple of chairs down from me - laying back after getting a shave - sat up and glared in my direction.

Have you guessed yet? It was the cop who had taken my punch. I don't recall him saying anything, but I do remember the look.

In the fall of 1971, I had one year left on my contract with the Kings, but I knew from the first day of camp that due to all my injuries, I was no longer in their plans. After I played out a very lackluster 1971-72 season in Springfield, my time with the team that had drafted me would come to a screeching halt.

I had been married in the summer of 1971. Now I was 22, a man without a job and no idea what I was going to do next.

But there was something in the air among hockey people: talk of a new league being formed. Most hockey people thought it would never get off the ground. Fortunately for myself and many other AHL players, the experts were wrong.

The World Hockey Association was formed by some guys who had a lot of money - or in some cases, pretended to have a lot of money. Their intention was to rival the NHL, so to gain instant credibility, they went after some big-name guys like Bobby Hull, Derek Sanderson and others with million-dollar contract offers.

Big Third Period Enables Amerks to Top Kings, 7-5

By GENE McCORMICK

The Springfield Kings were in hopes of taking over second place in the Eastern Division as they met the Rochester Americans Saturday night at the Coliseum.

Trailing, 4-2, going into the third period, the Amerks scored four straight goals to finish with a 7-5 victory.

Two new players were making their home debut for the Kings, both highly regarded by coach John Wilson. Al Johnstone was guarding the goal and Ed Hoekstra was skating at center. Both aided Springfield in beating Cleveland, 5-4, Friday night.

Two Games Each

The season series between the Amerks and Kings was squared at two games apiece, each having won at home twice. Although the Kings won their last meeting, 10-2, in a game which reached nearly riot proportions, the Amerks having been playing some of the best hockey in the American Hockey League over the past month. Coach Dick Gamble's charges were 5-1-1 in their last seven games and 6-2-2 in their last 10.

Goring Misses

Butch Goring missed a good chance to put the Kings on top in the first minute of play but shot wide of the cage from eyeball range. The Kings didn't do much thereafter although they managed to outshoot the Amerks, 12-10.

Rochester, however, clicked for a goal off the stick of Blackburn at 18.31. Red Armstrong and Garth Rizzutto assisted. Blackburn beat Johnstone from almost straight out with a 20-footer into the far corner. Armstrong was keeping Kings defenseman Brian Gibbons busy at the time and that allowed Blackburn an open shot.

The Kings got untracked in a hurry in middle session and scored four straight goals before the Amerk were able to collect their second of the night in the 16th minute.

Sharper passing led to the Springfield surge. Goring easily put away Jim Stanfield's goal-mouth pass at 1.12, after Doug Volmar started the scoring play which t'ed the score at 1-1. Murphy then put the Kings ahead at 7.28, after wrestling control of the puck away from a Rochester defender in front of the cage. He simply pushed the puck by Zimmerman's outstretched skate.

Westbrooke had plenty of time to shoot and accurately fired the puck by Zimmerman after taking Dineen's lead pass to score at 10.26.

Stanfield boosted Springfield's lead to 4-1 on the first power-play goal of the game at 11.41. Again, some nifty pass work by Roger Cote and Wayne Lachance got the puck to the puck into the far corner Stanfield who backhanded the puck into the far corner from 20 feet.

(Photo by Steve Lemonis)

Kings' Roger Cote and Rochester goalie Lynn Zimmerman follow flight of puck after shot by Springfield's Butch Goring was deflected by Zimmerman. Skating behind Goring is Kings' Gary Marsh.

★ ★ ★   ★ ★ ★

Rochester Player Goes to Court

A Rochester Americans' hockey player surrendered himself in District Court Saturday on a disturbing the peace warrant connected with a fight at a Springfield Kings hockey game Nov. 7 at the Eastern States Coliseum, West Springfield.

Neil G. Armstrong, 32, of Ontario, N.Y., was released on $50 bail, and his case was continued until Jan. 21.

The cases of a Springfield Kings' goaltender and trainer, charged with assaulting West Springfield policemen during the same incident were also continued to Saturday, Jan. 21.

Goalie Bruce N. (Boo) Landon, 21, of Kingston, Ont., and Peter G. Demers, 21, of Coach Lite Apartments, Agawam, the trainer, were charged with breach of peace and assault on a police officer.

Both Landon and Demers pleaded innocent to the charges Dec. 7.

Landon is accused of assaulting Patrolmen Anthony Cestavi and Michael Daniels, while Demers allegedly struck Patrolman Anthony Martilli.

Curtis Kodak All-American

JOHN CURTIS

Springfield end John Curtis and Trinity running back Dave Kiarsis were the New England players named to the Kodak College Division All-American football team Saturday.

The team, selected by the American Football Coaches Association, was announced here by Springfield College coach Ted Dunn, chairman of the committee.

Others in the backfield were quarterback Jim Lindsey of Abilene Christian and running backs Leon Burns of Long Beach State and Calvin Harell of Arkansas State.

Also on the offensive line were end Lionel Antoine of Southern Illinois, tackles Melvin Holmes of North Carolina A&T and Mike Potchad of Pittsburg, Kan., State, guards Sterling Allen of Wofford and Conway Hayman of Delaware and center Dub Lewis of East Texas State.

The defensive unit consisted of ends Henry Reed of Weber State and Lawrence Brame of Western Kentucky, tackles Dave Pureifory of Eastern Michigan and Vern Den Herder of Central Iowa, linebackers Gary Gustafson of Montana State, Ronnie Hornsby of Southeastern Louisiana and Pepe Papara of Wisconsin-Milwaukee, corner backs Bill Casey of East Tennessee State and Willie Germany of Morgan State and safeties Dwight Harrison of Texas A&I and Ron Stein of Montana.

Among those named for honorable mention were guard Bob Pena of University of Massachusetts and back Bruce Laird of American International.

**All-Western Mass.
Grid Squads ... Pages 66-67**

Those salaries were unheard-of at the time throughout pro sports and especially hockey, which had been a closed shop for decades with only six NHL teams (and about 120 big league jobs) until just a few years earlier with expansion in 1967.

But hockey was growing. Television had begun to take interest in the sport. The "Summit Series" between Team Canada (the first time the term "Team Something" was ever used) and the powerful, not-really-amateur Soviet Union national team was capturing the imagination of a larger audience.

With hockey markets expanding beyond their traditional bases of Canada and the U.S. Northeast and Midwest, it began to look as if the WHA had a shot.

The WHA owners thought so. They chased glamour names and filled their other slots with marginal NHL guys and some of the best players in the AHL. I was selected by the New England Whalers, who modern fans recognize from their future years in Hartford.

At the start of the WHA, though, the Whalers were going to play some games in the Boston Bruins backyard, the Boston Garden and also at the old Boston Arena.

At the same time, the Montreal Canadiens acquired my NHL playing rights. I received a call from Ron Caron in the Canadiens front office, and he tried to convince me the WHA would never get off the ground. Ron offered me a contract over the phone: I would get a whopping $16,000 if I made Montreal and $9,000 if I ended up on their farm team in Halifax, Nova Scotia.

I had grown up two hours from Montreal and I was still unemployed, so this offer was tempting. The only problem was they had a young goalie named Ken Dryden (the second future Hall of Fame goalie, after Billy Smith, to enter into my own future) so I knew my chances of making the Canadiens was slim.

I also did not relish the thought of telling my new wife that we were going to be living in Nova Scotia. Remember, I had promised not to take her away from her family to Canada. I turned the offer down.

Shortly after saying no to Montreal, I received a call from Jack Kelly, who was to become the coach and general manager of the New England Whalers. Jack asked me to drive up to Ottawa, Ontario to discuss a contract. It was a memorable offer that would serve as the beginning of what I consider to be the craziest but most enjoyable years of my playing career.

11
THE NEW ENGLAND WHALERS

Many books have been written and many stories have been told about the World Hockey Association. I have heard and been a part of incidents involving bounced checks, teams moving from hotels in the middle of the night because bills were not being paid, and a few of the other wild and bizarre stories about the League.

I remember the WHA being called the World Home for the Aged or the Worst Hockey Anywhere. However, I also know for certainty, that the very first championship team in 1972, the New England Whalers, could have beaten many of the teams in the National Hockey League. I was proud to be a part of that team.

Despite what people wanted to say about this new league, it changed the lives and the bank accounts of many players, coaches, trainers, and other hockey personnel. Today's young millionaire stars, many of whom have probably never even heard of the WHA, should be reminded that it was this league that started to give players leverage in salary negotiations. It was also one of the turning points in my life.

In 1972, very few players had agents to handle their contract negotiations. Most who did were the elite guys. But, when the WHA was formed, it was as if a new breed of "agents" came out of the woodwork, trying to capitalize on eager hockey guys who wanted to find their fortune in this new start-up league.

Some agents were not very trustworthy. Many did not have the credentials or the experience to handle contract negotiations. There are many documented stories about players who lost thousands of dollars because they trusted others to take care of their business matters.

Roof collapse of the Hartford Civic Center - January 19, 1978 - This is the way the Civic Center coliseum roof collapse looked from the 22nd floor of the Sheraton-Hartford Hotel. (Republican file photo).

Some players turned over their entire paychecks to agents who, in turn, gave the players a stipend to live on. The rest of the money was invested, and sometimes these investments disappeared.

I shouldn't generalize, though. There were a number of qualified, reputable, high-integrity agents who truly had the players' best interests at heart.

When I was drafted by the Kings in 1969, I'd never had an agent and I'm not sure it really would have mattered. However, with the new league and the prospect of dealing with a new team and management, I decided that maybe it was time to have someone represent me.

I was contacted by Charles Abrahams, who told me he was handling several of the new players that had been selected by teams in the WHA. He wanted to add me to his client list.

I never took the time, nor would I have even known where to start, to do my due diligence on his background. I was married and just wanted a contract, so I decided to give Abrahams the permission to handle things for me.

I had been contacted by Whaler coach and general manager Jack Kelly for Abrahams and myself to meet him at a hotel room in Ottawa. The first red flag should have been when there was another player in the room who was also negotiating his deal.

At that time, you never shared contract information with another player; it was considered confidential. I sat ten feet away from the other player, Terry Caffery, and listened to him talk to Kelly about how much money he was going to be paid. Charlie then sat down with Jack and after about three minutes, he presented me with a contact.

I was told it was their final offer, which made no sense because it was their first and only offer. So much for "negotiations."

In my last year in the AHL, I had been making $9,500 with the Kings, so the Whalers' two-year offer of $25,000 a year was a big deal. I noticed in the contract that there were no signing bonuses. When I asked my agent about this, he was unaware that goaltenders receive bonuses for wins, save percentage or other statistics. I ended up having my own discussion with Kelly, who provided me with a bonus clause.

With that, I signed my first WHA contract. I still had the sounds of the non-believers rattling around in my brain, warning that the league would never get off the ground and I might never see a dime of this nice contract.

The league opened play as promised in the fall of 1972. The Whalers were to play some games in the Boston Garden and others at the very old Boston Arena. I had proven myself to be a good backup to starting goaltender Al Smith, who had had NHL experience with the Pittsburgh Penguins and the Toronto Maple Leafs. That first year, we won the Avco Cup (the WHA's answer to the Stanley Cup) and

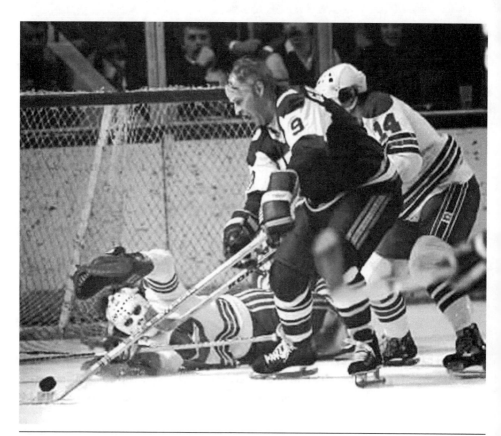

Hartford Whalers Gordie Howe moves in on this shot of the Winnipeg Jets goalie during this 3/22/78 game at the Springfield Civic Center following the roof collapse at the Hartford Civic Center. (Photo by Mark M. Murray, The Republican).

although I never played a game in the playoffs, I enjoyed every minute of it and especially the celebrations that followed. We knew how to party.

At the end of the year, Jack Kelly, wanted to extend my contract and told me I would not need an agent. I signed an extension that jumped my salary to $35,000, and $45,000 for the second year, along with some attainable bonuses. If you add on the $9,000 each player got for winning the Cup, my first year with the Whalers finally meant I had some money in the bank. It came at a time I needed it the most, because I was building a house and my wife was pregnant with our first child.

I paid my agent the money I owed him as per our agreement and thought I was done with him. But that was not to be the case. We met again when we were playing a game in San Diego and I was taking a pregame nap, because I was going to play that night.

There was a knock on the hotel door, and when I opened it, Abrahams was there. He said I owed him more money, even though I had not heard from him since our initial contract discussions in Ottawa and he'd had nothing to do with

Bruce Boudreau and Bruce Landon, Feb. 5, 1988. (Photo by Mark M. Murray, The Republican).

my new deal. I let him do his talking. Then I closed the door.

I never heard from him again. We got pounded badly that night and I had a really terrible game, which I blamed on the interruption of my afternoon nap.

During my five-year tenure with the Whalers, I was pretty much always the backup goaltender, first behind Smith and later behind a goalie from Sweden, Christer Abrahamsson. Being the backup to Al Smith was great because he was a warrior and you knew that when he started a game, he was going to finish it. Knowing that allowed me to enjoy myself the night before a game, probably more than I should have done.

Hell, I even went to a movie in the afternoon of a game if I knew I was not starting.

I always battled a weight problem while playing for the Whalers. When Smith was playing, I would wear a rubber jacket under my equipment and do stops and starts during warmups. Management loved it because they thought I was really trying to stay loose in the event I had to play. Actually, I was just trying to work up a good sweat, so I could justify the beers I was going to have with the boys after the game.

Above: Bruce Landon, goaltender of the New England Whalers, World Hockey Association. (Photo courtesy Landon Family).

Right: Bruce Landon making a save against a shot by Hockey Hall of Famer Bobby Hull. This framed photo is proudly displayed over Landon's mantel piece. (Photo courtesy Bruce Landon).

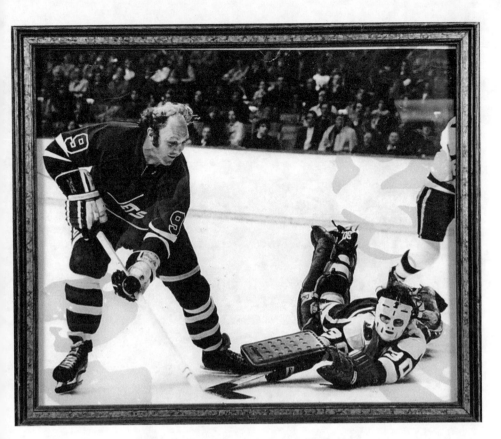

When I did play, Smitty was my biggest cheerleader. Al died at a very young age, only 56 when he passed in 2002. When I heard he was sick and did not have long to go, I called him at his home in Toronto. We had a brief conversation that he ended by saying, "Smitty has pulled a groin and you are going in, Batesy."

I hung up the phone and cried like a baby.

I got enough starts to prove my worth to the team, but I was always the second guy. Unlike a lot of goaltenders, I was able to go in cold when necessary and play well. I still relished the opportunity to play and when I had a good game, I wanted to keep playing. I loved Jack Kelly as a coach and as a man, but we had our moments, too.

On one occasion, Jack pulled me aside after practice and told me to get ready because I was going to start the next night in an important home game. The morning of the game, after we had just finished our brief morning practice, Jack called the team together at one end of the ice for his usual pep talk. He then turned to Smitty and said, "Be ready, Al, you are starting."

I was furious. I skated down the ice and proceeded to throw a temper tantrum. I tossed my stick about twenty rows into the stands, next went my gloves, and was getting ready to fire my mask as far as I could when I noticed Kelly coming down the ice. He could be very intimidating at times with his Whaler hat pulled down tight and a famous stare that could bore through you. I thought my days as a Whaler were over.

*Bruce Landon, Whalers' publicity photo.
(Photo courtesy Landon Family).*

LARRY KISH
COACH

Above: Whalers Coach Rick Ley [L], AHL President Jack Butterfield [Center], Gordie Howe [R] Whalers Special Assistant to the Managing General Chairman, July 12, 1990.
(Photo by John Suchocki, The Republican).

Right: Larry Kish, coach of the Springfield Indians.
(The Republican file photo).

Bruce Landon featured on the cover of volume 1 of the Harpoon: The Official Magazine of the New England Whalers for the 1972-73 season.

He came up to me and now we were face-to-face. He said, "Batesy, right now you are a backup goaltender, so just go out and be the best (expletive deleted) backup you can be." I had dodged a bullet, but it was not the last time my temper would get me into deep doodoo.

Life was not always easy for me with the Whalers. I was constantly looking over my shoulder and it seemed like every year, there was new goalie in camp, determined to take my job. Training camps were always stressful times and I never knew if I would be good enough to make the team.

Every year in camp, pictures are taken of the players for the media guide and program. For my five years with the Whalers, my picture consistently displayed a great big cold sore as my nerves would get the best of me.

As I look back now, I think dealing with the pressures of earning my place on the team helped me later in my management days. I never wanted to let anyone know they could do a better job than I could. Failure was not a word in my vocabulary.

The Whalers sent me down to the AHL a couple of times and when it happened, I always thought maybe it was time to retire. You have heard athletes say that when they get traded or demoted, it is always harder on the wives and families than it is on the player. This is especially true when your wife gets the news before you do.

During the 1973-74 season, we were on an extended two-week road trip across Western Canada, starting with a game in Edmonton, Alberta, when Kelly took me aside after practice on the first day of the trip. He told me since I had not been playing much after coming off an injury, they were going to send me to Jacksonville, Florida, which had a team that year in the AHL.

I couldn't figure out why they didn't tell me before the trip had started, but who was I to question a management decision?

Jack couldn't have been nicer about it in delivering the news. He knew my wife was pregnant with my second child, so he told me the Whalers would pay to fly Marcia and my daughter, Tracey, down to be with me. They had booked me on an early morning flight out of Edmonton to Hartford, where I would pick up my wife and daughter and fly down to Florida.

I had to arrange for a cab to pick me up at the hotel at 4 a.m., in Edmonton, where the airport is a good 45-minute ride from downtown.

It was ten degrees below zero when the cab pulled up, and so windy the snow was blowing sideways. I had two suitcases, all my hockey equipment and sticks. We were about ten miles outside of Edmonton when the cab broke down. With no cell phones in those days, the cabbie could not get in touch with dispatch to get another cab out in time to get me to the airport for my flight.

I was panicking. I got out of the cab and started hitchhiking. After about ten minutes, I was able to get a ride in the back of a pick-up truck from a mechanic who was on his way to the airport.

Robert J. Schmertz — Chairman of the Board
Howard L. Baldwin — President/Trustee
W. Godfrey Wood — Exec. Vice President
William E. Barnes — Exec. Vice President Marketing/Public Relations
John C. Giordano — Director

Robert P. Donovan — Director Media Relations
Bill Henderson — Sales Manager
Art Dunphy — Director of Publications
Michael Reddy — Ticket Manager
David Renwick — Asst. Ticket Manager

Jack Kelley — General Manager/Coach
Ron Ryan — Asst. General Manager/Director of Player Personnel
Jack Ferreira — Head Scout
Skip Cunningham — Equipment Manager
Joe Altott — Head Trainer

NEW ENGLAND WHALERS HOCKEY CLUB
Suite 705 Statler Office Building / Boston, Massachusetts 02116 / 617/357-9012

Pat Arseneault — Executive Secretary
Dianne Marshall — Coach's Secretary
Betsy Renwick — P.R. Secretary
Jackie Saltoun — Bookkeeper
Susie Stevens — Receptionist

Bryan A. Barber, MD — Team Physician
Robert C. Lincoln, DMD — Team Dentist

Minor Officials: Timekeepers — Tony Nota, Robert Henderson. Penalty Timers — Robert Henderson, James McDermott. Public Address Announcer — Weldon Haire. Official Scorer — Gerald McDermott. Statisticians — James McDermott, Saul Weiss. Goal Judges — Jack McGlynn, John Britt, John Ryan, Steve Cedorchuck, Steve McBride, Terry McLaughlin, Frank Kelley, William Riley, Bob Walsh. Penalty Box Attendants — Ed Gibbons, Mark Tully, Mike Donahue, Jack Donahue.

New England Whalers Management and staff, 1972-73 season. [From the Harpoon: The Official Magazine of the New England Whalers, 1972-73].

I had not yet told my wife that I was being sent down, since I wanted to do it in person rather than on the phone. It didn't matter, because the Whalers had released it on the 11 p.m. sports and Marcia happened to be watching. When I finally got home, I was able to soften the blow a bit by telling her she was coming with me.

The irony of this story is that the Whalers wanted me to go to Jacksonville to get some practice and playing time. The problem was that there was no practice rink. I played three games and never practiced once. I came back ten pounds heavier and with a horrible sunburn.

It is interesting that in all the years I have spent in Springfield, the only time I played at the Civic Center (now the MassMutual Center) was as a member of the Jacksonville Barons. That game ended my assignment to the AHL and I was recalled the next day. Yes, we beat the Springfield Kings on their home ice.

I was also assigned to Providence, along with teammate Tom Earl. It was supposed to be for only two weeks, and we were both told not to find a place to live. We could commute, or if necessary, they would put us up at the Holiday Inn.

The coach was John Muckler, who went on to great success with a number of teams in the NHL, including a long stint with the Edmonton Oilers. John didn't really like Tom or me, or at least, that was the impression we got. We thought he was ticked off because we were commuting. He didn't like the arrangement the Whalers had made with us, and he made that very clear.

On more than one occasion, he said if I was late for one practice, I would not only pay a big fine, he would make sure I would never get recalled. Every day, I would leave my home at 6 for the 90-minute drive to Providence - usually arriving before the trainers or any of the players. On game days, I would grab a room at the hotel next to the arena.

For the most part, the commute was uneventful, with the exception of the one time I had to drive to Logan Airport in Boston. I was going to meet the team for our trip to the Maritime Provinces in Canada.

We got nailed with a heavy snowstorm in the early morning of the day I was leaving for Logan, but there was no way I could miss the flight. I left my home at 4 a.m., to give myself plenty of time, but I was driving in a blizzard and traffic was moving at a snail's pace on the Massachusetts Turnpike. I was getting nervous, and I knew Muckler would have my hide if I didn't make it.

I decided to try to pick up speed, but I hit a patch of ice and did a 360 landing on the other side of the road, facing the wrong way. God must have been looking out for me because I somehow avoided hitting another car or the guard rail.

It left me an emotional wreck, but I was able to get to Logan on time, beating the bus that had to come from Providence with the rest of the players. I had the last laugh, because the only one who missed the bus was coach Muckler. He had not been able to get out of his driveway.

My only other minor league assignment from the Whalers came during the 1974-75 season, when they asked me to go to Cape Cod and play a few games. The Cape Cod Codders played in the old North American Hockey League and were coached by Larry Kish, who would later become a head coach in Springfield. I only played three games and not very well, but getting to know Kish was worth the trip. Larry was a great storyteller, and at times was known to stretch the truth a little bit.

In 1979, I would meet up with Larry again, after I had retired and was working in the Springfield front office. Kish was our head coach, having been given the job by the Whalers, who were leasing the franchise that year from George Leary.

My wife and I had him over for dinner one night. Sitting in our living room, Larry told us he had never been married and had no children. A few weeks later I found out the truth that not only had he been married, but he also had a kid.

I have no idea why he didn't want to tell us the truth, nor did I really care.

It was because of Kish that I got a chance to coach an American League game. It was early in the morning of a home game when I got a phone call from Larry, telling me he was really sick, and I had to go behind the bench. There were no assistant coaches at this time, and he didn't sound sick, but I was not going to question him.

We lost the game. For the record, in fact, I lost every game I coached, six in all.

My other coaching stint came when Springfield Indians coach Gordie Lane was suspended for five games for taking part in a very ugly brawl against Fredericton. I was asked to replace him. We lost all five games.

My good friend Bruce Boudreau, a very successful NHL coach, was a player on that team. Bruce reminds me about my bad coaching record every once in a while. I always respond by telling him it was those five games under my supervision that provided him with the knowledge he needed to enjoy his own coaching success.

For all five years I had with the Whalers, it seemed as if we had pretty much the same cast of characters and everyone had a nickname. I was Batesy, being named after former Toronto Maple Leafs goaltender Bruce Gamble, who was the original Batesy. On the first day of camp with the Whalers, I was stripped down to my underwear and Brad Selwood and Rick Ley - both of whom had played in Toronto - said I looked like the original Batesy.

That became my name. To this day. no one ever associated with the Whalers calls me by my first name.

To them, I am Batesy. Rick Ley was Plug. Selwood was Ragsy, Tom Webster was Hawkeye, Jim Dorey was Flipper, Paul Hurley was Shooter, Al Smith was Bear, Tommy Williams was Bomber and the list goes on.

The stories are endless with the Whalers. I have some great memories and some I would like to forget. There was the time I was almost killed by a can of Coke, for example.

We were playing a game in the brand-new arena in the Cleveland suburb of Richfield, Ohio. It was a massive facility that seated over 17,000 fans. I was starting in goal with Bob Whidden, who was subbing this night for Gerry Cheevers, in the other net.

The play had just left our end after I had made a good save. As the puck went into the neutral zone, I straightened up out of my crouch, but just as I did, a can of Coke hit the ice in front of me with such force that it took out a large chunk out of the ice.

A maintenance worker who was working during the game had been up in the ceiling rafters of the building. He had the can beside him and knocked it over. I wore a mask but never wore a helmet attached to it. If I had still been in my goaltending position, the can would have split my head open.

Every road game was an adventure and you can't make up some of the stuff that happened. We had landed in Toronto and were going through the airport when our coach, Ron Ryan (who had taken over for Kelly) collapsed on the floor of the concourse. Wayne "Swoop" Carleton, who was closest to him, got down on his hands and knees and started massaging Ryan's feet and ankles. The rest of the players had no idea what the hell he was doing.

But it worked because when Ron finally got up, he was fine and did not need further medical attention. When we asked Wayne what he was doing, he said, "That is what I do when my horse on the farm falls down."

On another long road trip, my wife decided to buy me a new suitcase. We were at the airport ticket counter and the guys started busting me because my new suitcase was the same color as the team's uniform. I told them it was one of those you can't break, and you see it on the commercials, where the gorilla is throwing it around.

To prove my point, I took a kick at the suitcase, only to get my foot stuck in the middle of it and make a big hole. The guys were cracking up and called over equipment manager Skip Cunningham to tape up my new "indestructible" piece of luggage.

I have mentioned how my temper has landed me in hot water more than once. One episode came when we were playing in San Diego and I got the starting nod. I played a pretty good game, but we were still beaten pretty badly.

I know for a fact that most of the guys had been out drinking pretty hard and did not get back to the hotel until about 4 am. I know because I had been with them. There was a rumor that one of the players had landed in Tijuana, Mexico and just made it back in time for the game.

After the big loss, I went in to the locker room and went into a rage. I broke a window, smashed a couple of water coolers, and put a hole in the wall with my goalie stick before the players cooled me down. Coach Ryan started yelling at the rest of the team, telling them he wished they cared about losing as much as I did. I was pretty impressed that he never said anything to me about my temper tantrum.

Nothing more was said, and I never told my wife - until my next paycheck arrived and I had a thousand dollars deducted to pay for damages to the San Diego locker room. I had some explaining to do that time.

All in all, I can't say enough good things about the Whalers organization and everyone associated with them. Even though there were plenty of problems with the WHA, the Whalers were first-class in everything they did. It started at the top with Howard Baldwin, who was one of the founders of the league and president of the Whalers. And it's funny how the hockey world works.

Many years later after I had retired and become part owner of the Springfield Falcons, Howard approached me about buying the franchise. That didn't happen, but Howard and I remain very friendly and I have a great deal of respect for him.

He was always great to me and my family and I love the guy for having the courage of his convictions and the guts to stand up to the NHL.

The WHA didn't make it to the 1980s, but its stronger franchises were absorbed into the NHL. One of them was the Whalers, who made Hartford a big-league city until the franchise moved to North Carolina in 1997. In the short time it existed, the WHA changed hockey forever. It changed my life, too, all for the better.

12
RETIREMENT FROM PLAYING

Once I finally hung up the skates and packed the pads away, I owe my entire management career to George Leary. Nobody had a greater impact on my post-playing days than he did.

George was a hard-nosed Springfield attorney who had purchased the Indians from the legendary Eddie Shore, with the help of local businessmen John Roethweiller and John Isenburg. There was no doubt who was in charge, and that was George.

I first met Leary when the Los Angeles Kings hired him to represent me in the legal proceedings that followed that famous brawl at the Coliseum. George saved my career at that time and several years later, he gave me my first front office position.

When I had been released from the Whalers after five years, I was not sure what the future would hold for me. I was married with two young children. I did not have a college education and other than having the gift of gab, I was not sure what I had in terms of other skills.

Due to all of my injuries and the fact I had no desire to move around the country just to play hockey again, I had reached the point of being uncertain as to whether I would even sign a contract, if one were offered. That all changed when I received a call from George, who offered me a contract to be his starting goaltender for the start of the 1977-78 season. At 28, I was still certainly young enough to keep playing.

In the summer, Leary wanted me to do some sales work for him. It was an offer I could not refuse. The money was not great, but it allowed to me live in my home in West Springfield, and I was excited to have the chance to play for Gary Dineen, whom George had hired as his coach.

Above: Steve (L) and Jeff Carlson a.k.a. the Hanson Brothers from the movie "Slapshot" ham it up with 9-year-old Tim Gleason of Auburn at the Casey Park Arena in Auburn, Jan 23, 1999 "Region 1"
(Photo by Jim Commentucci).

Left: George Leary, Springfield Indians owner, Mar. 30, 1979.
(Photo by Kevin Twombly, The Republican).

Gary and I had been teammates for two years and we had become friends. He had an exceptional hockey mind and I sensed that he would be a good coach.

The added bonus for me was that I would be able to see what kind of salesman I could become. During my playing career, I had always volunteered for as many personal appearances as I could get, and I especially enjoyed public speaking.

Looking back now, that first summer of sales work and the ability to generate revenue would prove to be invaluable to me in later years.

My last game as a professional goaltender came as a member of the Leary-owned Indians in December of 1977. We had a game in Binghamton, and my brother and a couple of cousins drove down from Kingston to watch me play. They did not see much.

Early in the second period, I was pitching a shutout when a Binghamton player came down the left side and took a wicked slap shot that clanked off the crossbar. The red light never went on, but the referee ruled it a goal even though I know the puck had hit the bar and never went into the net.

When the referee went to speak to the goal judge, I lost my temper. I picked the net off the pegs and pinned the referee against the boards. He threw me out of the game and as it turned out, I would never play a game again.

Not exactly the last playing memory a player would want.

The next day in practice, Leary had brought in a player named Jeff Carlson on a tryout. Carlson was the brother of Jack and Steve Carlson, and the brothers became immortalized in pop culture for their role as the Hanson brothers in the enormously popular hockey movie, "Slap Shot." (Steve and Jeff played Hanson brothers in the 1977 movie that featured Paul Newman as the star. Jack Carlson was supposed to play the third brother in the film, but he was called up to the NHL. The third Hanson brother was actually played by a guy named Hanson - Dave Hanson, another player who logged time in the NHL and WHA.)

With Jeff Carlson in our practice, the team was doing a very simple line-rush drill, but Jeff did not stop in front of the net. He bowled over the top of me with my knee twisted underneath him.

I was carried to the dressing room with what would become my last injury as a player. Rather than being bitter, I find it funny that a guy who ended my playing career wound up starring in one of the best cult movies ever made. It also started me on a long and productive career in management - the next chapter of my life and one that would benefit me for decades.

George was already aware of my sales skills, as I'd had great success in the summer selling program ads for him. He offered me a chance to recuperate, rest my knee and have surgery if necessary - or go into the front office. It was a no-brainer.

Even though I was only 28, I had undergone shoulder surgery and the injury had

Top: Craig Patrick [L] Rangers' general manager, and George Leary, owner of the Springfield Indians at the Springfield Civic Center, Oct. 7, 1981. (Photo by Michael Gordon, The Republican).

Above: Harry Sinden [L] with Springfield Mayor Theodore Dimauro [R], 1981. (The Republican file photo).

never healed properly. I had a badly sprained Achilles tendon. I had smashed both thumbs, ripped my finger twice and had a couple of concussions.

The front office looked appealing, so I made an easy decision to call an end to my playing career. At one time, I had been labeled one of the best young goaltenders to come out of Canada. I do wonder if I would have lived up to that billing, had I been able to stay healthy.

I got along very well with George, even though he could be one of the most intimidating men I have ever met in my life. I think it was from my backbone to stand up to George that I really learned to have the courage of my convictions. I think I also earned his respect because I did not cower away from his bullying.

George may have been as tough as nails, but he was also one of the funniest guys I've known, especially at times he used his famous one-liners. His sarcastic tongue could cut through a 2-by-4, and I was on the receiving end of it more than once.

One day, he came over to watch practice and the guys were not on the ice. It was the 1981 season, we were a New York Rangers affiliate and George had hired Tom Webster as our Coach.

Our team was in last place and when George saw the guys not practicing, he went crazy, especially when he saw the players taking turns on the exercise bike. He came flying into my office shouting "We could win the (bleeping) Tour De France, but we can't win a hockey game."

Even though I was not officially the general manager, George ordered me to speak to Webster. It was not an easy discussion; Tom was a good friend and had been a former teammate of mine with the Whalers. But I did it.

On another day I was busy in my office making sales calls, working on statistics, and doing press releases and all the other chores that kept piling up on my desk. George came into the office and told me to grab my coat, for I was making a trip with him.

He had straw all over his sports coat and he looked like he'd just rolled around in the barn. We went out to his truck and I was told to take a seat next to a lady who looked as if she'd just crawled out from under a rock.

George told me she was a client he was representing on a drug charge. By the way she looked, I never thought he would win that case.

We were heading out to his farm. One his horses had fallen down and could not get up, so George, myself and this drugged-out woman - who could not even keep her eyes open - were supposed to pick the horse up. Thankfully, as it turned out, when we arrived at the farm, the horse was up and running around like it was getting ready for the Kentucky Derby.

Thanks to George I also had a chance to attend my first AHL Board of Governors meetings. As was customary with Leary, no notice was given. He just showed up at the office and told me we were going to Boston. I think he just liked having company.

There were only about seven or eight people at the meeting being run by Jack Butterfield, the AHL president. The governors included Harry Sinden from the Boston Bruins and Sam Pollock of the Montreal Canadiens.

Growing up in Canada, I was in awe of these guys. Sinden had once played for the old Kingston Frontenacs in my hometown and as a kid I used to go and watch those games. Harry later became known for leading the Bobby Orr-Phil Esposito Bruins, and Pollock was the architect of several Stanley Cups won by the Montreal Canadiens.

Butterfield was doing his best to control the meeting, but things started to get out of control when Leary and Pollock got into a heated argument. When George got mad, he had this big vein on the side of his head that started to blow up. This time, it looked like it was going to explode.

George got out of his chair and was screaming, "What the hell do you know about hockey, Pollock?"

It didn't matter to Leary that this guy was responsible for putting together the best teams that had ever played in Montreal. We left the meeting without another word being said.

When the team was not playing well, George took it out on everyone around him, especially coaches. He fired Gary Dineen during the 1977-78 season and replaced him with Bob Berry. In 1978, he hired Ted Harris to be our new coach, but fired him during the season and replaced him with Peter Stemkowski.

It was the Harris hiring where George showed that if he had the mind to do it, he could really stick it to somebody. George hated it when local sportswriters Gene McCormick or Sam Pompei, who wrote for the Springfield Newspapers, would get a scoop and print it.

McCormick wrote for the morning paper, the Union. Sam was a sportswriter for the evening paper, the Daily News. In the fall of 1978, George prepared to announce the hiring of his new coach, so he arranged for a big press conference at noon in the Brooks Building, in front of the Coliseum.

George really wanted to make sure word did not get out, and he especially wanted to make sure McCormick didn't get the news early, which would have let it appear in the morning paper on the day of his big announcement. But Gene was doing his job and sniffing around for the scoop.

In the week leading up to the event, George had interviewed Doug Carpenter for the job and booked him a room at the Marriott Hotel. But he was not going to hire Carpenter for the job. McCormick got wind of this and called the hotel to confirm that a Doug Carpenter was registered.

On the morning of the press conference, the Springfield paper led with the headline that Doug Carpenter would become the new coach of the Springfield Indians at noon that day. I will never forget the look on Gene's face when he came swaggering into the Brooks Building, thinking he had the scoop of the century.

Instead he looked like had taken a dagger to the heart when he saw myself and George talking to Ted Harris, who was being introduced as the new coach.

I loved George for the opportunity he gave me. I loved his sense of humor, even though it could be hurtful at times. I loved the lessons he taught me on how to stand up for what you believe in.

I saw the dark side of George at times, but I have better memories of the good moments. Most of all, George gave me a second chance after I quit on him to move to Florida to operate my worm farm.

13
THE WORM FARM

When I speak about George Leary, who gave me the chance to step right into the front office after my retirement as a player, I have so many great memories. I also have some painful and embarrassing memories of this time in my life. But they were equally important in the shaping of my life as it took the next turn.

Hockey players and professional athletes in general are not always the most wise and savvy investors. I know, for at one point in my life, I fell into that unfortunate category.

Whether it's something to brag about or not, I'm an expert on worms. You don't meet a worm expert every day, and there are reasons for that. But no Bruce Landon story could be complete without at least some acknowledgment of the worm farm.

I was working for George as his director of marketing and public relations and had saved a little bit of money from my Whaler playing days. My wonderful in-laws had moved to Florida, after they'd given up fighting with West Springfield town officials in their attempt to build a nine-hole golf course in West Side. Cy, my father-in-law, was a builder by trade but he also had this idea of buying a worm farm near Deltona, Florida where they had relocated.

After discussing it over with them, I decided that maybe this would be a good investment for me as well. I'd already owned a small piece of property where I thought one day, I would build a house. After reading a few articles about worm farming, I really thought this was going to be the next big thing, so I plunked down $10,000.

That was a lot of money in 1978, especially for me. With this investment, I now owned over three million worms in a little farm not far from my property.

My wife and I then decided we would sell our house, move to Florida and live with her parents while we built our own home and I would work the "farm." Two days after we made the move South, I really started to think I had taken too many pucks to the head.

What in the hell was I doing? Was I crazy? It was the middle of July and about 100 degrees in the shade. On the first day out to the farm, Cy had to slam on his brakes as a huge rattlesnake was crossing the road. That alone should have been enough to send me packing.

My job was to feed cow manure to the worms, keep moving them around and watering them. The worms were in long troughs, each about 50 feet long and the heat, along with the smell of the cow dung, made me want to vomit. But I stuck it out, at least for a short time.

Why buy a worm farm? It sounds absurd, but actually some good reasons do exist. Do you use a high-end fertilizer for your garden? If so, read the ingredients; it may say worm castings. Worm poop is one of the best kinds of fertilizers you can buy. A lot of people won't believe it, but worms are also edible. If you Google it, you can find different recipes that use worms. Worms are also used in some parts of the country to eat and clean up landfills. Both the male and female worm reproduce, so there's never a shortage of the little creatures.

What sealed the deal for me was that I read that Lucille Ball owned a large worm farm in California. If it was good enough for Lucy and Ricky, it was good enough for me.

We lasted about two weeks. We hated the summer heat in Florida and I really started to hate worms. Also, at the time, my youngest daughter, Tammy, needed an eye operation and we wanted it performed by the doctor back in Springfield. With my tail between my legs, I called George up and asked him two questions: could I have my job back, and could we get our house back? He never hesitated about giving me my job back. I really think that deep down, he knew I would be back.

As for the house, George had no idea, but he said he would find out for us. We had agreed to sell the house to an older couple, but we had not closed on it. They heard my story about Tammy and I think he felt sorry for us, so they agreed not to pursue the sale. I have no idea what happened to my three million worms, but hope they were fed to some hungry fish off the coast of Florida. Over the years, I became the target of a lot of jokes about my worm farm investment. Believe me, I've heard them all.

Did I have a big sign that read "Welcome to Landon's Worm Ranch?" How did I find such a small branding iron? Did I have names for all of them? On and on it went.

From that bizarre experience, I became very cautious where to invest my money, except perhaps the time I was going to buy the Orange Julius franchises in Springfield. There was also the time I was going to buy an old movie theater and convert it into racquetball courts. At last, some 15 or 16 years later, when the opportunity came along to invest in a hockey team, it was a no-brainer, even though I did not have the money.

I am happy to say at least one of my brilliant ideas worked out, but I continue to dream about what the next big business adventure will be. Playing in the game is a lot more fun than being on the sidelines.

14
COONEY BUYS THE INDIANS

In 1979, Springfield Indians owner George Leary asked me to oversee the hiring of a new broadcaster. We were looking for someone who could also do sales in the summer, and also handle some statistical work.

After going through several resumes and audio tapes, I decided to hire a young man named Peter Cooney. Little did I know at the time that he would go on to make his own mark in Springfield hockey history - including the 1990 and 1991 Calder Cup teams, the last of seven Springfield championship clubs in the 20th Century.

Peter and I would become very good friends and we had a great working relationship. He was a very funny guy, but also very eccentric.

About two minutes after meeting him, I knew he'd come from a family of wealth. The first sign came when he pulled into the office parking lot, in what appeared to be a brand-new BMW.

I knew what George was paying him because I'd done the contract, and there was no way it was enough to afford that kind of ride. Peter had also settled into a great apartment that was on the higher end of the rent spectrum at that time.

I learned very quickly that Peter was extremely guarded about his background. He never wanted people to know he had money. His parents, who I'd had the opportunity to meet on a couple of occasions, were wonderful down-to-earth people who lived in Attleboro, Mass.

The only two people Peter really trusted were his accountant, Dennis Fusco, and his lawyer, Gerry Coogan. I got to know them very well over the years and we struck up a good friendship, but they always knew how much they could share about Peter and how little he really wanted people to know about him.

*Peter Cooney (L) and Bruce Landon (R), 1982.
(The Republican file photo).*

In time, this friendship ended rather abruptly after Peter sold the Indians and I struck out on my own to purchase a new franchise. That would come 15 years later. None of this was on any of our minds at the outset of our relationship, of course.

After purchasing the franchise from the Kings, Leary decided to move the team from downtown Springfield back to the legendary Eastern States Coliseum in West Springfield for the start of the 1976 season. To do that, he had negotiated a terrific deal, which also gave him the concession rights. That's actually where the money is - in food and beverage, not so much in just owning a hockey team.

But, badly needing a prime tenant, Springfield Civic Center convinced George to move the team back again across the river for the start of the 1980 season. In doing so, they not only gave him concession rights for the AHL games, but for every event in the building.

During his short tenure as owner, Leary changed coaches and affiliations and he was not an easy man to please. Eventually, I believe he not only got tired of the business but saw a great opportunity to sell the franchise.

Some points in my life are as clear as crystal. Others will always be foggy. But right down to the color of the briefcase, I remember when Peter walked into my office with George. All Leary said was, "Meet the new owner of the Springfield Indians."

I was surprised but not shocked. For my professional career, Cooney's purchase of the team was the best thing that could have happened.

Peter named me general manager of the franchise for the start of the 1982 season. I will always be grateful, for it gave me the opportunity to become more involved in the hockey side of the business.

I was able to get involved in player contract negotiations and work closely with the NHL teams. For the first time, I started to find out more about Peter Cooney, as a person and as an owner of one of the most storied franchises in the American Hockey League.

The "Cooney years" spread from 1982 until 1994. It was 12 years of both failure and great success on the ice, but not necessarily at the box office.

The back-to-back Calder Cups in 1989-90 and 1990-91 will be remembered as some of the best hockey ever played at the Springfield Civic Center. It was a source of great pride for me as general manager, and for Peter as owner. However, the real story is not about the results on the ice, the records in the yearbook or statistics of any kind. It is about the people that made it all happen.

It is about those front-and-center and those behind the scenes during a 12-year ride that for me was funny, sad and at times downright ugly.

It all begins with the guy in charge, Peter R. Cooney - and the stories are countless.

History of Hockey. The Springfield area's first professional hockey team dates back to this picture of the original Springfield Indians of 1936-1937 season. (The Republican file photo).

Top: Springfield Indians goalkeeper Kay Whitmore makes the save during a practice session at the Springfield Civic Center, at left is teammate Mikael Andersson, May 6, 1991.
(Photo by Dave Roback, The Republican).

Above: Coach Fred Creighton [Center] talks with Springfield Indians owner Peter Cooney [L], and New York Islander general manager Bill Torrey [R]. (Photo by Don Treeger, The Republican).

Springfield Indians coach Jim Roberts, Sept. 29, 1988. (Photo by Mark M. Murray, The Republican).

Above: Springfield Indians goaltender, Jeff Hackett. (The Republican file photo).

Right: Springfield Indians players hoist the AHL Calder Cup after winning the deciding game of the 1990 championship series, May 18, 1990. (Photo by Mark M. Murray, The Republican).

Springfield Indians player Joe Day raises the 1991 Calder Cup in front of the Springfield Civic Center, May 26, 1991. (Photo by Michelle Segall, The Republican).

Most people thought Peter was very tight with the dollar, but when it came to taking care of his players, he would spare no expense. When we were in the Calder Cup playoffs, for instance, we carried a lot of extra players. This was the side of Peter Cooney people didn't see.

Without being asked by NHL management or by our coach, Jim Roberts, Peter decided to rent two charter buses to transport the team. In the playoffs, the American Hockey League reimburses teams for standard travel costs, which includes one bus and per diem and hotel costs for 22 players.

The extra bus, extra per diem and hotel costs came right out of Peter's pocket. It was a great gesture that showed the players he was willing to do whatever it took to help the team win.

For every playoff series, he would take the entire team out to dinner - not just players but coaches, trainers, broadcasters and even the two bus drivers. It was always at a great restaurant and there was no such thing for Peter as a limited menu.

After games, he would take myself, the coaches and trainers out for a post-game meal and as many beers (or in Peter's case, vodka and orange juice) as we could drink. But the one thing you never did was tell Peter Cooney how to spend his money.

One year, broadcaster Bob Galerstein found that out the hard way. Peter had asked me to reach out to the group and tell them he wanted to take everyone to dinner. When the waitress came around to take our orders, Galerstein in his deep broadcaster's voice bellowed out, "Well, Peter, since you are picking up the tab, I will have the most expensive steak on the menu."

I knew right then we were in trouble. Cooney didn't say a word, but when the bill came, Peter grabbed it, threw down 50 bucks and said that should take care of his portion. Then he got up and left the table.

It took every dollar he had and some he had to borrow for Galerstein to pay his portion of the bill. It was a lesson well learned for those at the table.

Peter was a very bombastic guy at times, and although some of it may have been for show, he always created a scene in the press box during a game. In the best manner of George Steinbrenner, he was known to throw or smash phones if he didn't like a referee's call. More than once, he fired a couple of chairs off the back walk - not caring who or what was in the way.

However, the best of all came during the last game of the regular season as we were getting ready for the playoffs. We had worked all day in the box office, sorting out playoff tickets for all of our advertisers, knowing we had to deliver them the next day.

For whatever reason, Peter had brought them up to the press box and put them beside him. Sure enough, during the game, the referee made a call that sent Peter over the edge. He went ballistic and started pounding the table.

He hit it so hard, in fact, that to this day I can still picture about 500 tickets flying off the counter and floating like confetti at a ticker tape parade down to the fans below us. That was Peter Cooney.

He hated to fly and traveling with him by plane was never a great experience. One playoff series was against the Cape Breton Oilers in Nova Scotia. We had a charter flight on a Dash 8 that only held 54 passengers and we were flying out of Bradley International Airport in Windsor Locks, Connecticut.

To keep costs down, the charters we chose flew out around midnight. We left on a bus after our home game and headed to the airport in a pretty good wind and rain storm.

I was sitting next to Peter on the bus. He was white as a sheet. He kept staring out the window and it looked like he was going to throw up.

Remember that in those days, we never had to go through security, so the bus pulled up next to the plane. The small Dash 8 had ropes tied to cinder blocks, and it was swaying back and forth. It was raining so hard that we had to wait on the bus for about an hour before we could board.

I could see the panic in Peter's face when he knew we were actually going to get on the plane. We had so much equipment and personal luggage that a lot of the hockey gear had to be stored in the back, which eliminated some seats, so guys had to double up.

I slid into my seat. Peter piled in next to me and the sweat was beading up on his forehead. After a couple of minutes, the pilot - who truly looked like he was 15 years old - came out of the cockpit with a calculator in his hand.

He said we had too much weight on the plane, so he had to get everyone's weight, then add that to the estimated weight of the equipment and the fuel to determine how much weight would have to be eliminated before we could take off.

That was it for Cooney. He screamed at Coach Roberts not to lie about his weight. He also told the pilot that he weighed 230 and I was 190, but it didn't matter - we were getting off the plane.

By now, it was about 3 am., and we were back on the bus that had not left the tarmac yet. We returned to the Civic Center, slept in the office for a couple of hours and made arrangements to take a commercial flight that got us to the game in time.

Obviously, the charter made it. But from what we were told, it was a very rough flight. Even in times of success, the business posed great challenges for Peter - and for me.

In the 1989-90 season, we won a Calder Cup as an affiliate of the New York Islanders. At the end of the season, the Islanders pressured Peter to renew for another season with them, but they also wanted a big increase in the affiliation fee.

Peter refused to sign. We continued to explore our options, one of which was signing with the Hartford Whalers. The problem that year was that the Whalers had their AHL team in Binghamton, New York, and it was a last-place team with only 16 wins.

The AHL's annual meeting was in Bermuda that year, and league President Jack Butterfield was getting pressure from the other owners to get Peter to make a decision. Peter and I were wrestling with how we could sell it to the fans and the media that we were dumping the Islanders - our partner for a Calder Cup champion - with a last-place team to replace it.

The first day of the meetings ended at noon, so we could all have time to enjoy the beach and the other amenities of Bermuda. I had gone for a swim in the ocean and was sitting on a raft about 50 yards offshore when I saw Peter - who is not a small man - wading into the water and then swimming out to see me.

As he pulled his big body up, all he said was, "Can we make it work?" I knew what he was talking about, so we sat for about an hour in the blazing sun, figuring out how we could convince our fans that the proximity of the Whalers in Hartford to Springfield would help us in player assignments.

It was on that raft in the ocean at a Bermuda resort that the decision was made to dump the Islanders and sign a new deal with the Whalers. It was that Peter Cooney decision that wound up giving us our second Calder Cup.

During the "Cooney years" we had a chance to watch some great coaches and players hone their skills before going on to outstanding NHL careers. In Jeff Hackett and Kay Whitmore, we had award- winning goaltenders who backstopped two Calder Cups. We had some of the toughest players ever to lace on a pair of skates, and I always thought Peter enjoyed the fights more than the games. He was a big wrestling fan who could name most of the WWE "entertainers" at the time.

More than anything, we enjoyed some great working relationships with NHL teams and the general managers and assistant managers who dealt with us on a regular basis.

The one man who stood out was the late Bill Torrey, the architect of the Islanders 1979-83 dynasty and the man personally responsible for giving us the players we needed to win our first Calder Cup. Torrey also provided us with the man who, for me, was the best motivator as a coach I have ever been around - Jimmy Roberts.

Everyone who follows the AHL knows the success Jim had on the ice by winning back-to-back Calder Cups in Springfield, with two different NHL affiliations. It's time they knew just some of the things that went on behind the scenes with Coach Roberts.

Life with Jimmy was never a dull moment, and it started the first time I met him. Hired by the Islanders to be Springfield's coach, he got my call to congratulate him and extend an offering to help, in any way I could, to get him settled in Springfield. Our first conversation was memorable.

"Brucie (he always called me Brucie), wife Judy and I need a place to stay for a couple of days. We are bringing our trailer with us, so I won't need a hotel, but need a place to park the trailer." No problem, I told him. He could park it in my driveway.

The next day, Jimmy showed up driving one of the biggest motor homes they make. It had to be about 48 feet long. He hooked it up to my electricity and that is where they lived, not for a couple of days but for about two weeks until they were able to find a house.

Every morning, I would wake up at 5 a.m. to the smell of Jimmy's cigar as he would be sitting out on my deck, having his first coffee of the day.

One day, we had a game in Portland. We used to go up on the day of the game, which meant we had to leave about two in the afternoon.

The bus pulled up to load up the equipment, but the driver was so sick he couldn't function. We did not have enough time for the bus company to send us another driver, so Jim abruptly said, "We're not waiting, I will drive the bus."

With his trademark cigar, he got behind the wheel and away we went off to Portland. We won the game and I can still picture Jimmy with a beer beside him, driving us home and telling stories all the way.

We did not want to get anyone in trouble, especially the driver, who was passed out for about six hours in the back of the bus, so I never told the bus company until many years later. They did not find it as hysterical as we did.

More memories: during one stretch of the season, we were in a terrible slump. Jimmy called me in my office and screamed at me, "Brucie, get over here. I need your help. We need to shake things up."

He'd taken a pencil and written all the players' names on little pieces of paper. He then took off his old woolly tam, threw the names into the hat and told me to start picking names.

As I picked out a name, Jim would write it down on his pad. It didn't matter if it was a defenseman or a forward - whoever I picked out was going to play together. We started the game with a defenseman at center and two forwards on defense. We won the game in a blowout. As the saying goes, "Whatever it takes to win".

Jimmy Roberts won five Stanley Cups as a member of the Montreal Canadians in the 1960s and 1970s. Hockey Night in Canada, every Saturday night, was must-see TV for every Canadian fan from coast to coast.

Peter and I never realized what a celebrity Roberts was until one year when we went to the NHL draft in Montreal - many years after he had retired as a player.

Cooney and I had never been to the Chez Paree, a world- class gentlemen's club and Jimmy wanted to take us. As we were walking up the street, everyone was either shaking his hand or yelling out his name like he was a big-time movie star - and to some people in Canada, he was.

As we neared the club, a line that stretched for about two city blocks. Peter and I told Jim to forget it - we'd just grab some dinner. But Jimmy told us to follow him.

We walked by all the people in line and the Maître D' started shouting, "Monsieur Robert, Monsieur Robert." Before we knew it, we were not only in the club but in the best seat in the house.

Personally, I hate pulling rank or using my connections in the hockey world for anything, but I have to admit that this time, it was worth it. The first-class "strip club" lived up to its reputation.

When asked why he thought everyone remembered him many years after he had played, Jimmy said, "Brucie, look at this puss. It is not the prettiest thing in the world, but it was plastered all over television for many years. Who in the hell would forget it?"

Jimmy was a great coach. He was never much of an X's and O's guy, just someone who knew what buttons to push - though sometimes, he could push the wrong ones, even with me. He had a fiery side and I have been known to have the odd temper tantrum myself, so it was inevitable that we would have our blowouts.

It happened a couple of times. Once, I was sitting in my office one day when Jimmy called me on the phone from his office and started griping about something pretty stupid. He hit a nerve with me and I went flying out of my office across the ice and barged into his office.

Springfield Indians fans and players celebrate their victory in the 1991 Calder Cup game at the Civic Center. (Photo by Don Fontaine The Republican).

He was sitting with his feet up on his desk puffing away on that big cigar. I got right in his face and started yelling at him. I said, "Don't interfere in what I do, I don't tell you how to coach."

He jumped out of his chair and I thought punches were going to be thrown. He then smiled, put his arm around my shoulder, and said, "Brucie you are right, let's go have a cup of coffee." It was this side of him that made him such a great coach.

The players just never knew what to expect from him.

We could lose three straight games and the guys would think they were going to be bag-skated. Instead, he would give them a short, 30-minute practice.

Or, you could be on winning streak and he would skate the guys until they practically dropped.

His practices were always upbeat as he would stand in the center of the ice with his famous tam cap on, a pair of old cream-colored winter mittens on (with the fingers cut out) and a whistle around his neck that he never used. He just barked out orders - and the guys knew what to do.

Dale Henry, one of the players during our Calder Cup run, told me after a tough practice, "I hate that guy. But I would go through a brick wall for him."

The only other time I had a pretty good beef with coach Roberts had to do with a coaching decision, one with which I had trouble agreeing. I was the GM and although most player decisions were made by our NHL club, we had agreed that we would sign a couple of our own players. With Cooney's support, I worked hard at getting Bruce Boudreau signed (a story by itself that I will touch on later).

Bruce came in and did everything you could ask of him, including winning the AHL scoring championship during the 1987-88 season when he racked up 116 points in 80 games. The following year, the team was not very good, we were about 50 games into the season, and Roberts told me he was going to sit Boudreau out and limit his playing time.

Peter and I had trouble swallowing this news. Not only was Boudreau still leading our team in scoring and was far and away our best player, we were paying him a pretty good salary to play, not sit in the press box.

I lost my temper and told Jimmy that was ridiculous. Boudreau was our best player. He was a fan favorite. How could we tell our dwindling fan base that the only guy worth paying to see would not be playing?

In addition, Bourdreau had a lot of pride and we knew it would kill him to sit out. We argued for about two hours, but it was a battle I knew I was going to lose, so I told Jimmy I was going to trade Boudreau.

I called Gabby (Boudreau's nickname) into my office and told him what Jim wanted to do. As expected, he did not take it well. I told him I would trade him if it was what he wanted.

He was having a few family issues, who that year had stayed at their home in St. Catherine's, Ontario. With an AHL team in Newmarket, outside of Toronto and not far from where he lived, I told him I would see if I could work out a deal to trade him close to home, so he could be with his family.

I called up Gord Stelleck, who was running the Newmarket team, and explained the situation. Stelleck was shocked because Gabby was one of the best players in the league and he wanted him badly, but he but was short on players and had nothing to give up.

But I had made a promise to Gabby, and I was not going to renege on it and let him down. Our team was not going anywhere, so getting a lousy player in return was not going to help. I traded Boudreau for future considerations, which really means you were getting nothing in return.

All we did was save some of his salary for what was left in the season. That is how Bruce Boudreau became the only player in Springfield hockey history to win a scoring championship one year and get traded for nothing the following season.

Boudreau and I have remained long-time friends. I'd like to think my loyalty to him in 1989 is one of the reasons why.

Jimmy Roberts could not only get the most out of every player, but he also had an incredible eye for talent. During our first year together, we were affiliated with the Islanders, and a young defenseman named Bill Berg was struggling so much that, without telling anyone, he left the team and returned to his home in Toronto.

Jimmy and I met to figure out the best way to deal with the situation. I wanted the Islanders to call Berg and threaten to suspend him without pay if he didn't return. But Roberts lobbied for a different approach.

"Let's give him some time to be with his family, think things over and then I will give him a call," Jimmy said. "However, when he comes back - and he will- I'm converting him to forward."

Bergie was a great skater and very smart, but he put too much pressure on himself when playing defense. The rest is history. When Bill returned he became a defensive forward, and he went on to a pretty good NHL career with over 500 games.

Did Jimmy Roberts save Berg's career? Almost certainly, yes.

Berg wasn't the only example by any means. That same year, I received a call from Steve Carlson, who was coaching Johnstown in the ECHL. Carlson had a small, skilled forward named Greg Parks who was too good for that league, and Steve told me we should call him up.

We were looking for another forward, so I called Parks up to give him a chance. At his very first practice, I was standing by the bench and about 20 minutes into the drills, Roberts skated over and told me the Parks kid might be the best player on our team.

Parks went on to put up 54 points in 49 games. He was also outstanding in the playoffs with 22 points in 18 games, and he was instrumental in us winning our first of two straight Calder Cups. The talent that might have escaped the eye of others was apparent to Jimmy's watchful eye from the start.

Jimmy never watched video, but his office television was always on. I have never believed in coincidences and I believe things happen for a reason, and I was always intrigued by how Roberts' TV was always tuned to the channel that showed nothing but falcons nesting at Monarch Place in Springfield. He was mesmerized by those birds.

Fast forward about five years. When we bought our new franchise after Cooney's Indians had been sold and moved to Worcester, it ended up being named the Falcons - after those same birds that had captivated Roberts on TV.

Jim Roberts was one of a kind. He passed away at 75 in 2015 - too young, because to the end of his life, he had so much to offer. His passing was marked by the St. Louis Blues, for whom he had played, when the team wore "JR" decals on their helmets for a time.

He played in three All-Star Games and scored 320 points in 1,006 NHL games, even though he played defense as well as forward. I have nothing but great and wonderful memories of him, and I will always be thankful for how he was the driving force behind our back-to-back Calder Cups in 1990 and 1991.

Most of all, I enjoyed his friendship, his sense of humor and the lessons he taught me on how to deal with players in a direct and honest approach.

Over my own long career, I take gratitude and pride in knowing that to the best of my knowledge, I did not burn any bridges. That's tough to avoid when you are negotiating contracts, leases and affiliation agreements, voting at league meetings and firing and hiring staff members. There are times when disagreements became confrontational, but for the most part, they should never become vindictive.

The one exception to this involved my dealings with Peter Cooney as his control over hockey in Springfield was nearing its end.

It bears repeating that I have always been grateful to Peter for naming me general manager in 1982, and I had the pleasure of working for him for 12 years. But in 1994, things took an ugly twist when Peter announced he had sold the Indians to Roy Boe in Worcester - shortly after I made my own announcement that I was going to try keeping hockey alive in Springfield.

Peter's public statement about the sale immediately made him public enemy number one with the media and fans who could not believe Springfield, which had been an AHL member almost continuously since 1936 (with one brief interlude in the 1950s) was going to lose its team. After my news about going forward to try saving hockey, I was portrayed as the good guy wearing the white hat, the guy who was charging in to save the day.

This did not sit well with Peter and his team, which consisted of Gerry Coogan, his lawyer, and Dennis Fusco, his accountant. Fireworks erupted between our lawyer, Frank Antonucci and Coogan after a deal involving transfer of the team name had collapsed.

We had reached an agreement on a few issues and were going to be given the right to use the Indians name, a legendary part of Springfield hockey history that we had no plans of changing. That didn't last long after Coogan got involved, and he presented us with a laundry list of requirements with which we had to comply, before they would allow us the rights to the Indians moniker.

It ended up with Antonucci telling them what they could do with their list. We would go forward with a new name, which wound up being the Falcons. The Indians name was never again used in Springfield hockey, even as ownerships changed over the years, and a quarter century later, it's safe to say it never will be.

Nowadays, of course, there is some debate over Native American nicknames, but it was (and to old-time fans, still is) a beloved name and Springfield tradition that never caused a problem and gained us widespread recognition. What happened in the negotiations was a shame, but no team name was worth having our hands tied as we were getting our new, AHL expansion franchise off the ground.

After the news had broken, Peter and I never spoke. However, I did receive a call from his wife Ann, who ironically, my wife and I had set up for Peter on a blind date many years earlier. This was no friendly call. For about an hour, Ann tore into me about how I was ruining their lives, and how I had destroyed Peter's master plan. I guess it did not matter to her that I was unemployed, or that Peter had angered everyone from city officials to fans of Springfield hockey with his decision to sell the team.

It was Ann who told me what Cooney's long-term plans were - which even today, few people know about. Cooney's plan was to let the city go for a year without a franchise, and then buy another team and bring it to Springfield. He felt during this year without hockey, fans would really miss it and appreciate it, and they'd be begging for another team to return to the Civic Center ice. He also felt he would then be able to negotiate a new much more favorable lease with the building. My announcement put an end to this.

Truth be told, it would have never worked. I was told more than once that if Cooney was part of our ownership group, we would not get a lease. Over the years, he had unfortunately destroyed his relationship with city officials, with his constant threats to move the team if he did not get his way.

Peter once went public stating that he was putting up his own building off Interstate 91 near Enfield, Connecticut. However, the property he was looking at involved wetlands, which meant nothing could be built on that site.

Peter had also taken me on a couple of trips to the Olympia in West Springfield, which was home to some college and high school teams with limited seating to see if that building could be renovated enough to house a professional team.

As a businessman who was losing money, Peter had every right to look at all options - unfortunately, even if it meant selling the franchise. Maybe, just maybe, if he had shared his so-called plan with me, I would not have gone forward with mine. I also would have forgotten about the way he had delivered the news to me that he had sold the team, even though it was a bitter pill to swallow.

After I received a call from his lawyer telling me I was going to fall flat on my face, because there was not enough time to pull it off, I became more determined than ever to make it work.

It took us only two weeks to get our ownership group in place and form our business entity, Pro Friends Inc. In that time, we were also able to negotiate our lease, arrange for an NHL partner and apply for a new franchise with the AHL.

All of this was big news in the media, which further put a major wedge between Peter and myself. We went from being good friends to never speaking. Unfortunately, Peter's wife Ann passed away and I never did have another conversation with her after that one phone call.

For a few years thereafter, Peter and I never spoke, and it bothered me deeply. Even though I should have been really upset about the way he handled me when he sold the team, in time I came to realize that I should have expected nothing differently. Even though he was less than truthful with me when I asked him if he was selling, I am sure he had a reason not to say something at that time. As I have said before, Peter kept all his business dealings close to the vest.

What upset me most is that after he told me he was not selling, I turned down two very good job offers. Ed Anderson, who owned the Providence Bruins at the time, had offered me an opportunity to run his franchise for him.

In addition, long-time friend Tom Turley, who owned the Turley Publications printing firm, had made me a great offer to leave hockey and become his sales manager, with an opportunity to grow his business and explore new revenue streams. That came only one week after Peter had told me he was not selling.

It was a Thursday night and I was soaking in my hot tub, when my wife handed me the phone and said Peter was on the line. He said very little, but I remember it word for word.

"Hi Bruce, it is Peter, I have sold the team, I will see you in the morning," he said. The next day, it broke in the news so at least I got the courtesy of the call before it became public knowledge.

Peter went on to become a very successful player agent. It was through his new career that the ice was finally broken between us.

I had gone on to run the Falcons and Peter badly wanted to have one of his clients signed. At the time, we were working with Phoenix and young Taylor Burke was their Assistant General Manager. Taylor had left the Springfield signings up to me.

Every time Peter called Burke, Taylor told him he had to call me. Finally, in the best interests of his client, he had to call. It was an awkward few minutes of conversation, but I never carry a grudge, we never brought up the subject of the Indians sale and we have not done so to this day. You can't live your life looking through the rear-view mirror.

Peter and I worked closely on some player signings right up until I retired. He is a very good agent and I have recommended him to several young players looking for someone to represent them.

With Peter, I could call any time of night, which usually happened when you were searching for a last-minute replacement from the ECHL. There was one night when we were in dire need of a defenseman, it was well after midnight and I put a call into Peter.

Driving back from somewhere in a bad snowstorm, Cooney pulled over to the side of the road and we talked about our needs. He said he would get back to me. Within an hour, he'd arranged for one of his clients to leave his ECHL team and drive to Springfield.

Peter did warn me that the guy was not one of his best, but at least he was available. Peter never - and I mean never - hung up the phone without pitching one of his guys to me. That is what makes him a good agent. He cares about his guys.

I can't emphasize enough that I have nothing but respect for those people who are willing to put their wallets on the line. Peter was one of those guys. In many ways, his way of doing business was totally opposite to how I wanted to do things, but at the end of the day it was his money and he had the right to make all the final decisions.

American Hockey League President David Andrews at press conference in Springfield, Dec. 22, 2010. (Photo by Mary M. Murray, The Republican).

15
MY RUN FOR AHL PRESIDENT

A lot of things were happening during the 1993-94 season. Not only were talks of the Indians' sale heating up, but long-time AHL president Jack Butterfield had announced he was retiring. The league naturally formed a search committee to find Jack's successor.

The committee was made up of franchise owners, including Peter Cooney, who owned the Indians, and Thomas Ebright who then owned the Portland Pirates. Butterfield called me and told me he wanted me to run for the job, and that he would support me. I was flattered, but never felt I was the right person for the position. I was the general manager of Springfield, but other than my playing days and my work in sales, my resume for this type of responsibility was not really that strong.

Still, after discussing it with my family, I decided to throw my hat in the ring. I had nothing to lose and it was, after all, a very high-profile job in the sports industry. Even so, I was never sure I even wanted the job.

I think now that in the back of my mind, I was doing it out of fear the Indians would be sold and I'd be out of work altogether. From what I was told, there was a pretty strong list of candidates, but I made the early cuts as the names were whittled down to three finalists.

That meant I had to go through a very lengthy and extensive interview with Tom Ebright. I didn't get the job, but I heard several years later that I had made it down to the final two. The finalists had been myself and Dave Andrews, who had a very extensive background in hockey, not only as a player and coach but on the business side as well.

Unlike me, he was also a college graduate, having attended Dalhousie University and the University of British Columbia. Andrews got the job. There's no question the committee made the right selection.

David Andrews was absolutely the perfect person for the job, and he has proven it time and time again over 25 years. He guided the league through some turbulent times and took it to record growth in attendance, with expansion from coast to coast. Once a league restricted to the Northeast United States and eastern Canada, the AHL now serves the entire North American continent.

I have always been a big Andrews fan, and I've been able to watch first-hand the wonderful job he has done. He was still going strong as the 2018-19 season unfolded with no end in sight.

Whoever replaces Dave - whenever that would be - will have big shoes to fill.

I have said many times that I don't believe in coincidences. Things happen for a reason, and the events that kept me from becoming AHL president are one of the best examples of my life.

Just a short time after Andrews was selected, I was able to become president of my new ownership group that helped save hockey for Springfield. I was officially presented with the certificate of ownership from Dave Andrews, and it still hangs on a wall in my home office. It always will, a reminder that things do happen for a reason.

16
THE FALCONS ARE HATCHED

The fact that we were able to purchase a new franchise in such a short period of time is still fascinating to me, and I am sure that not many people know the real story of how it all came together. From start to finish, the entire process made me realize there are some people in the hockey world you can trust with a handshake, and others where you had better have your ducks in a row - and then pray like hell that nothing went wrong.

It all started with one phone call from my very best friend and former teammate, Wayne LaChance. Wayne was sitting at home, watching the news on TV-22 when he saw my interview before the last Indians game, where I got bold and said I was going to try to keep hockey alive in Springfield.

It was a pretty gutsy statement for a lot of reasons. I had no clue at the time as to how I was going to pull it off. I had no money, no partners and no plan, but I knew deep down that somehow, I would find a way.

Wayne called me the next morning and asked me one very forward question: Did I think we could make it work?

I have always believed in having the courage of your convictions, and I told Wayne that if we stuck to a solid business and marketing plan, we could make it work.

I remembered that about two weeks before Cooney had announced he was selling, I had presented him with a 20-page report on everything from financials, to staffing, to sales.

It was something I had worked on at nights for several days. Peter took it home but the next day, he came into my office, threw it on my desk and simply said he would do it his way.

From left, Lyman Wood, Peter A. Picknelly and Bruce Landon announcing at a Aug. 9, 2002 press conference at the Sheraton Hotel, the transfer of ownership of the Springfield Falcons hockey team. (Photo by Michael S. Gordon, The Republican).

The first day Wayne and I got together, I pulled the report out of my desk and gave it to him to read. His response was what I expected.

"This is great, Batesy (my old hockey nickname). Let's get started and make this happen," he said. We were underway.

The AHL had told us we would have to buy an expansion franchise, which at the time seemed to make no sense because Springfield had had an American Hockey League team since 1936. The league was asking for $750,000 as the expansion fee.

When you buy an expansion franchise, you also get territorial rights, but for us, the rules changed. The league wanted us to have a franchise, but it was not like skating in on an open net.

First, the AHL had to carve out a special territory for us, which gave us some limited protection but certainly not the 50-mile territorial rights that other teams had as part of their deals.

Wayne and I had to put a group of investors together quickly. We were already in to early April, and the league had given us a deadline of their spring meeting in May to make our presentation.

We figured that we had to come up with at least a million dollars to cover the expansion fees and to give us some operating capital. The only way Wayne was interested in doing this was for the two of us to have controlling interest so that we could run the franchise the way we wanted.

Above: Flanked by Don and Judy Bridge on his far right, Bruce Landon on his right and Peter A. Picknelly to his left, Lyman Wood speaking at the Aug. 9, 2002 press conference announcing the transfer of ownership of the Springfield Falcons hockey team. (Photo by Michael S. Gordon, The Republican)

Right: Bruce Landon of the Springfield Falcons at the Springfield Civic Center rinkside, Oct. 2, 1996. (Photo by Mark M. Murray, The Republican.)

Wayne's first call was to his long-time friends Don and Judy Bridge, who owned Bridge Manufacturing in Enfield and the Enfield Twin Rinks, the business Wayne was running for them and one he eventually bought. They agreed very quickly and put their trust in us - along with their checkbook. They would become part of the ownership group, but we still had a long way to go.

Don wanted to set up a meeting with a man named Lyman Wood, a very successful businessman with whom he was friendly. The problem was that Lyman knew nothing about hockey or the guy who was going to run the franchise.

When we met at Lyman's office with Don and Judy, I knew that in making my presentation, I was only going to get one kick at the can. Lyman was (and still is) a big advocate for the city of Springfield, and I had to convince him this was a good deal for the city.

I have to add that Lyman has one of the best mathematical minds I have ever come across. Years later, I found out he was an avid card player in big-stakes games. I didn't know that at the time, but during our meeting, he put on his best poker face.

When I had finished my presentation, which to this day may be the best I have ever made, he just stared at me without saying a word. I thought we were kaput. He then said the words that radically changed my financial life forever.

He simply stated, "I am in, if you are in." His reasoning was that he did not know me or anything about the hockey business, and he would invest only if I had skin in the game as well.

I had never planned on being an investor because I did not have the money. However, again being bold and full of moxie - what some people call chutzpah - I told him he had a deal. We walked out of his office knowing we were making progress, but I was not ready to celebrate yet.

I had an important phone call to make. I had to break the news to my wife, Marcia.

It went something like this, "Hon, I have some great news and maybe some not-so-great news. Lyman is in, but I have to come up with a (boatload) of money."

That was quite a statement with all sorts of potential impact, but there was no pushback from her, nor has there ever been. I was fortunate at the time to have a very small mortgage, but that changed quickly as I had to take out a second mortgage to come up with part of my investment. The rest would come in the form of sweat equity.

OK. We now had Lyman, along with Wayne, myself and Don and Judy, who were going to own the majority interest in the franchise. We also had our lawyer, Frank Antonucci, and our accountant, Phil Shuman, who combined had a very small interest, but importantly, provided their services. But we still needed more.

When word hit the streets that we were in the process of building our investment team, I received a call from Peter Picknelly Sr., who wanted to meet with me. He offered to invest some money, which was very generous of him, since it was the first time we had ever met. He just loved our city and knew that it was the right thing to do.

I just didn't think he would be the right fit for us, though, so I respectfully turned him down, even though we still needed one more investor. In the meantime, the clock was ticking toward the May 4 league deadline.

The day following my television interview, I had also received a call from a New York lawyer named Stuart Levy. He had happened to have been in Springfield at the last Indians game, and was back in his hotel room, watching the news, when he saw me stick my size-10 in my mouth by saying I wanted to keep hockey in Springfield.

Stuart wanted to meet with me, but would be traveling to England, so it would have to wait. With the deadline approaching, I basically dismissed the idea that it was going to happen.

A few days after we brought Lyman on board, he called to set up a meeting with his client, a guy named Tom Roberts. Wayne and I had never wanted anyone from

Chris Kellogg of WMAS-FM's Kellogg Krew, Springfield Mayor Domenic J. Sarno, and Bruce Landon of the Springfield Falcons were bartenders at the "Celebrity Bartending" fundraiser at The Student Prince / The Fort in Springfield on Nov. 4, 2015. Local politicians, civic leaders, and media personalities stepped behind the bar with all tips and a portion of the evening's purchases benefiting the Springfield Symphony Orchestra.
(Photo by Dave Roback, The Republican)

outside the area, but we were not stupid, either. We needed money, and soon.

We never did know where Tom's money came from, but his check cleared the bank and that was all that mattered. During the entire time Roberts was involved with us, we only saw him once in Springfield.

In two weeks, we had our investors and formed our company which was called Pro Friends, Inc., which was Wayne's idea. We were ready to make our presentation to the league.

As part of the deal, we also needed an NHL affiliation to provide us with players. I was in the process of working out a deal with the Whalers, but to hold us over, I had my good friend Roy Mlakar, a long-time AHL guy in Cleveland, Providence and New Haven who was running the Los Angeles Kings make a commitment to me. By sheer coincidence, that was the same organization that had drafted me as a player a quarter-century earlier.

Roy sent me a letter stating he would provide me with players if needed. That was good enough for the league.

Wayne, Shuman, Antonucci and I met in a hotel room in Boston to put our final thoughts together and review how I was going to make our presentation to the AHL Board of Governors. We got the call and Wayne and I went before the board, then returned to our room. We thought we had a deal.

Another lesson I've learned, though, is to never assume anything when money is on the line. Cooney still owned the rights in Worcester (where the Indians had moved) and Ed Anderson owned the Providence franchise.

After we left the meeting, they somehow convinced the league that they were entitled to a territorial rights fee to the tune of $250,000. I knew at the time this was totally ridiculous and unfair, but I had no time to fight them. I was called down from the room to meet with Anderson, who told me unless I came up with the other $250,000, our deal was dead.

Was he bluffing? Who knows? I think they thought we were going to fold and back out of the deal, which would have kept hockey out of Springfield, a turn-about that would have helped Cooney with his so-called long-range plans.

I returned to the room to give my group the news. At first, Wayne wanted to tell them to shove it, but little did Cooney and Anderson know that we were a little sharper than they thought we were. I was actually prepared for a little negotiation and had built up a cushion to go as high as $1.5 million for an all-in deal.

Why? I had always known there were other cities lining up for AHL franchises. I had told our group that once we got the franchise, if it did not work out and we were losing money, we could sell it for $2 million and even though there would be no hockey in Springfield, we would get our money back.

I called Anderson, told him he had a deal and that he could tell the Board. Finally, the call came from the league for me to go back down to the meeting.

With unanimous approval, we were granted our franchise to begin play for the 1994-95 season. I went back to the room to tell the guys. I will never forget Wayne's reaction.

"What the (hell) did we just do?" is all he said. (Well, it was actually a little stronger than that.) We had a franchise, but with no name and a whole lot of work to do in a very short amount of time.

After delivering the news of the sale of the Indians franchise, Peter Cooney had told me he would give me two weeks' severance pay, which I found to be a bit of a slap in the face. However, I was forging full steam ahead with putting things together for our new franchise, so I forgot about it. During my last two weeks with Cooney and the Indians, never once did I spend one minute of time on his nickel to work on the yet-to-be named new team.

I worked well past midnight every night. Sometimes I pulled all-nighters. Those early lessons from my youth and teen years about the value of hard work were coming in handy now.

To get going, we had to start thinking about a staff. We wanted to hire a very sharp, dependable person to become our business manager, and it was Wayne who suggested Bob Oliver, my nephew and someone both Wayne and I really liked. It had to be Wayne's decision as I did not want any kind of nepotism to enter in to our hiring decisions.

At the time, Bob was working for a big accounting firm in Hartford, but as we found out, he hated his job. We met at my kitchen table and told him we were rolling the dice, but we wanted him to be part of our team. On the spot, Bob accepted the position. The next day, he walked into his old job and gave his notice.

Our next order of business was for Bob and me to start working on a budget. At the time, I had no computer skills and for that matter, no computer. Bob still had access to one at the accounting firm. So quietly one night, during a big dinner party at my house, we left and drove to Hartford, and spent the entire night crunching numbers.

All the time we were there, I had one eye on the computer and another one on the door, expecting security to boot our butts out at any time.

In the meantime, we started to get pressure from media and fans as well as the AHL, to come up with a name for the new team. Originally, we planned on just calling it your New Springfield Indians, until the debacle that took place between ourselves and Cooney's lawyer, ruling out a transfer of the name from his old team to our new one.

Moving forward, we launched a name-the-team contest in conjunction with the Springfield Newspapers, where fans could cast their votes. According to the newspaper, it was the most well-received contest they had ever run.

Truth be told, the name that garnered the most votes was the Springfield Rifles. That had some local history of Springfield's manufacturing past attached, but we just did not see that fitting in with our marketing plans to create a family atmosphere and did not think, even then, that it was politically correct.

Our goal was to attract as many fans as possible, not risk appealing to some while alienating others over a team name we wanted everyone to share.

The name "Falcons" was a close second and the decision was made to go with it. It was named after the birds that had built their nest on the Monarch building in downtown Springfield. An old friend of mine and graphic artist, Frank Carter, designed our logo.

I didn't really like the name, but something strange happened that changed my mind.

To get some interest building, we planned a major press conference at Tower Square in downtown Springfield to unveil the new logo and jersey designs. At the time, we were renting office space on the 14th floor of their office building and our windows overlooked the Monarch building.

Five minutes before I was to make the trip downstairs to deliver my speech to a large crowd that had gathered, I was staring out the window and the peregrine falcons swooped right down in front of me. If the window had been open, I would have been able to reach out and touch them.

It had to be an omen that the name was right, whether I liked it or not.

Wayne and I were not wealthy, and we did not have a blank check from the other owners. We had to make this work. We had given ourselves a two-year time frame and if we lost money, we would be forced to put the team up for sale.

Local banker Don Chase had given us a $100,000 line of credit, but we never had to use a dime of it. The first year, we broke about even despite a lousy team. From that point on we made money, enjoying great success at the box office.

To this day, I really think it was a combination of some new, creative marketing ideas, promotions and the fact that fans wanted to support a couple of old former players who were doing their best to keep hockey alive in the city. As the years passed, we had some decent teams and were able to take attendance in Springfield to an all-time high - even higher than the old Indians teams at the Coliseum during the team's so-called "golden years" had drawn.

We created a family atmosphere within our office, and although we ran with a small staff, everyone did whatever was necessary to make things work. Over my years, both as Wayne LaChance's friend and business associate, I learned a great deal from him.

One of the first business lessons he taught me was to remember that our staff needed to be rewarded for their hard work and dedication. When we were enjoying good years, we used to host team Christmas parties with all the staff, their spouses and all the players and coaches at the Hofbrahaus in West Springfield. Wayne and I would have a surprise for our staff.

We had taken cash and placed it in envelopes, and at the end of the night, when it was just the Falcons' family together, we passed out the envelopes. When our employees saw what we had given them, it brought tears to their eyes. Wayne and I cried our eyes out as well, but that was nothing unusual for the two of us. It was something I will never forget.

During this party, we saw one of our players, Frankie Leroux, who was drinking a bottle of Opus One with a straw. We really didn't care. It was time to celebrate and we knew how to do it up right.

Our business and marketing plan was paying off. Our balance sheet was solid, and we were making money every year. I was having the most fun I had ever enjoyed during my business career. But as they say, all good things come to an end.

Once again, I stuck my neck out to make a very bold move. It was the 2001-2002 season and as I looked into the future, I did not like what I was seeing. The landscape of the AHL was starting to change. Costs for line items that were out of our control were starting to rise. Our building was also about to undergo a major renovation, which meant we would be playing in a construction site.

There were major issues with crime in downtown Springfield and I had a sixth sense that attendance was going to start dropping. The NHL partners started focusing more on player development than they did about winning, and it was only a matter of time before poor teams would eat away at our fan base.

I called Wayne and told him we had to sell. He was shocked by my decision because we were still enjoying financial success, but I owed it to the guy who had always believed in me when many others didn't. I convinced him that the timing was right to put the team up for sale.

I had somehow convinced myself we could turn our million-dollar investment into a huge windfall for Wayne and the other partners. Once again, Landon had stuck his neck out, and now I had to deliver on my promise.

But my ultimate goal was to make sure that the team stayed in Springfield.

A number of cities were looking to purchase an AHL franchise, and that was the leverage I had to use. I never expected it to be easy, though, and I was spot-on there.

One thing I never did during my entire career, at least to the best of my knowledge, was to burn bridges. Those relationships came through when I started the process of finding new ownership.

I had met Joe Cambi when he owned Springfield Food Service and I was pedaling sponsorships for the Falcons. I met with Joe and gave him my sales pitch. He was not an easy sell, but he agreed to purchase a 25% equity stake in the company if I could find the rest of the money.

My goal was to find four equal partners. Doing that would allow me to cash out.

While I negotiated in Springfield, several other cities had their sights set on the AHL. New arenas were up in Austin, Texas and Kansas City, Missouri, where their operators were looking for a prime tenant.

I had a healthy profit-and-loss statement, a mayor, Mike Albano, who did not want the team to leave the city, a soon-to-be-upgraded arena and no problem in finding an NHL affiliate, so I put the price tag at the unheard-of number of $5 million. At the time, no AHL team had been sold for more than $3.5 million.

Word got out that the franchise was for sale, and once again, I received a phone call from Peter Picknelly Sr., a strong supporter of the city. He told me his son, Peter Jr., would join our investment team.

I don't think Peter Jr. was thrilled when he got that news from his father. Peter was an avid supporter of Springfield but knew nothing about hockey or the business. I really didn't care because I had another 25 percent and was halfway to my goal.

Lyman Wood, one of our original investors in Pro Friends Inc., had agreed to remain - but again, only if I would keep skin in the game. He did allow me to sell

Joe Cambi In the warehouse of the Springfield Foodservice Corp, Sept. 3, 1998. (Photo by David Molnar, The Republican).

off 8 percent of my shares, so I did walk away with some cash. It was agreed that Lyman, along with myself and Don and Judy Bridge (who had also agreed to stay on board) would together bring another 25 percent to the Company.

That was three of the four. I was still short.

During the time I was pounding the pavement and looking for more money, I had several local people kicking tires, but none wanted to pony up the money. I met with the MassMutual Financial Group, which did not want to see the team leave the city but also did not want to be any part of ownership.

I finally made the call and used the leverage I had that swung things in our favor. I had received a call from an NHL team that wanted to buy the franchise but were going to relocate it. I put a call in to Mayor Mike Albano and told him point-blank that if we did not find another 25 percent, I was going to have no choice but sell the team.

Mike had always been supportive of our efforts. In 1995, he had torn up our lease to give us a better deal, and I knew he did not want to see hockey leave on his watch.

He was able to convince MassMutual to kick in the other 25 percent stake we needed, and I had my ownership group in place, but no contracts had been signed and another sales pitch had to be given.

We agreed to meet at the boardroom of the Sheraton Hotel. All the potential investors and their legal representatives were there. Prior to the meeting, I had agreed to lower the price to $4.5 million to show them how much we really wanted to keep the team in Springfield. I wanted the group to know that it was not just about the money for us.

It was time for Landon's dog-and-pony show. I had to convince this group of well-heeled local businessmen why this franchise was worth that kind of money. They asked us to lower our price even more, but I dug my heels in and simply said that Kansas City was willing to pay us more.

We would be taking too big of a haircut to drop the price further, I said. I will always remember the hush that fell over the room. Wayne said nothing and was stone-faced throughout. I was sweating it out and hoped they did not call my bluff and call someone in Kansas City. Finally, one by one, they took a vote and agreed unanimously to buy the team from Pro Friends Inc., for an incredible amount of money.

I was asked to stay on as president and general manager. After everyone else had left the room, it was just Wayne and me. We hugged and maybe cried a little. Wayne had just become a millionaire at age 55 and no one was happier for him than me.

As for myself, I had lived up to my promise to keep hockey in Springfield and make sure the investors received a nice return, not just on their investment but their belief in me as well. I also had a little cash to invest and was about to embark on our new entity, Springfield Pro Hockey LLC.

Indeed, what happened next would be several very turbulent years, to put it mildly.

Wayne LaChance.
(The Republican file photo).

17
WAYNE LACHANCE

Wayne LaChance and I first met at the Los Angeles Kings training camp in 1970. It was my second year as a pro and his first, and it began a lifelong friendship that went from the ice as teammates to the business, and throughout our personal lives as well.

Wayne had graduated from Clarkson University, where he'd had an outstanding college career. We both wound up being assigned to Springfield at the same time, and I had a car, so Wayne asked if he could hook a ride with me to Springfield.

We hadn't been on the road for ten minutes when he told me I was going to let him off in a little town called Hoosick Falls, which was on our way. He wanted to visit his girlfriend, Roxy, whom he would later marry. First, though, we were going to stop at a hamburger joint he liked.

It was only 10 o'clock in the morning, but over about three burgers each and five hours together in my 1970 'Cuda convertible, we forged a friendship that has lasted almost 50 years.

Everyone thinks that the Falcons came about because of Bruce Landon, but I know for certain that had it not been for the support and belief that Wayne LaChance had in me, hockey in Springfield would have been long gone. No story or book can be told about the start of the Falcons franchise, without serious attention to Wayne and the role he played, even if - and perhaps especially if - it was behind the scenes.

Wayne was and is my best friend, my confidante in so many ways, my business partner and teacher, my former golf partner, my racquetball opponent and a guy who has always known just what to say at just the right time. We shared so many laughs and good times, but moreover, he was able to be the strong voice and the calming influence when I needed it the most.

During our first few years of operating the franchise, Wayne was still running his other two businesses, the Enfield Twin Rinks and the Springfield Olympia. With his great business mind, he looked over our finances with Bob Oliver, our business manager, while I took care of the rest of the operation. It was with Wayne's help that I learned to understand profit-and-loss statements, and how to prepare a budget. Through him, I also gained the confidence to present business plans to our various investors over the years.

More than anything, Wayne understood me and what made me tick. He was never one to get very rattled over wins and losses, small crowds or those moments when things seemed to be coming unglued. Unlike me, he was always positive and upbeat and always able to find the silver lining.

Wayne also sensed when I was uptight and needed to unwind, something he allowed me to do many times.

One such night occurred at the AHL All-Star game in Wilkes-Barre, Pennsylvania, where our host, Jeff Barrett, threw a lavish party at a beautiful mansion. There were three floors with an open bar on each, and enough food to feed a small country. This came at a time when our team was really struggling, attendance was soft, and I was taking a lot of criticism from media and fans.

Wayne knew how much it was bothering me. I had made a decision to try breaking the world record on how much Scotch one 200-pound man could consume in one night, and it was not a pretty sight.

During that entire evening, Wayne did not drink. Rather, he was there to watch over me to make sure I did not make a complete fool of myself. He finally cut me off, but not until I had consumed sushi for the first time, which was not such a great idea since I am allergic to a lot of seafood.

Too much booze, though, can give you a great deal of courage. Wayne made sure I got back to my room safely. He did everything but tuck me in.

There's another part of that story he has never known, because I never had the nerve to share it with him. After he left me in my room, I was not ready to call it a night, so I slipped out of the room in my underwear and found some leftover pizza on a plate in the hall.

I decided to make a room-service call to Howard Dolgon, the owner of the Syracuse franchise and a man I'd seen earlier in a room near mine. Around 2 am., I knocked on Howard's door, standing in my boxers with a half-eaten pizza on a platter. That's when he made his mistake. He let me in the room.

I didn't know he had "company" at the time. Howard and I are great friends and I think it really started that night in Wilkes-Barre.

Wayne LaChance and I have a lot in common. We like to golf, we enjoy our Scotch, beer and good food and we enjoy time with our families. Throughout the Falcons days, we had a lot of laughs.

Springfield Mayor Michael J. Albano congratulates Bruce Landon and Wayne LaChance. (The Republican file photo).

    If you can't enjoy yourself when you're around Wayne, you just don't have a pulse. One example: every year, the league would hold its annual meeting at Hilton Head, South Carolina, where it was a combination of business and plenty of time for other activities.

    One day, we'd finished our meetings around noon and Wayne, his wife Roxy, my wife Marcia and myself decided to spend the afternoon on the beach. Wayne and I were sitting beside each other, wearing our dark shades and just shooting the breeze about the meetings, while the ladies were next to us.

    During this idyllic moment, Wayne gave me an elbow in the side and whispered for me look at what was coming toward us. It was a Bo Derek lookalike who was wearing almost nothing but a smile. We stared at her for what was obviously far too long, when Wayne noticed Roxy was giving him the stink-eye. Without missing a beat, Wayne yelled out, "Yeah, but can she cook!" Classic Wayne, a winning one-liner at just the right time.

    I learned a lot of valuable lessons from Wayne. He always believed everyone had the right to make a profit and made sure I remembered that in all my negotiations on leases, affiliation agreements and other contracts. In dealing with staff, he reminded me on more than one occasion that it's fine to take the staff out for drinks, but to buy them one or two and then leave. I was their boss. I wasn't to become their drinking buddy.

I was always the guy conducting the press conferences and giving the speeches, and Wayne was always in the background, but that is the way he wanted it. Everyone who cared about Springfield hockey, though, should know this: Had Wayne LaChance not made that first call to me on a night in April of 1994, I have no idea what direction my life would have taken.

Hockey is still in Springfield, and not just because of me. So many thanks go to that humble, smart fun-loving guy from Espanola, Ontario - even if you'll never hear it from him.

18
SPRINGFIELD PRO HOCKEY LLC

From the very start, I should have realized that the new ownership group was very passionate about keeping professional hockey in Springfield, but they were so diverse in their ideas about everything from marketing to business decisions that at times, we were almost dysfunctional. I take the blame for not taking more command of the situation. I should have done a better job of keeping everyone on the same page.

The ownership consortium did stay away from the hockey side of the business, which was good because as investors, they had every right to complain about things - especially considering that for many years during their ownership, our teams were downright terrible. The investors were all very, very successful businessmen and had made it very clear from the beginning they did not want to lose money. Unfortunately, that was not the case.

When I had told Wayne LaChance in 2001 that it was time to sell the team because of my concerns about rising costs, changes within the league, construction issues with the MassMutual Center and a fan base that was not growing quickly enough it was as if I had glanced into a crystal ball that revealed the future. All my predictions were coming true. Combine all of this with very bad hockey teams, and it was a recipe for financial disaster.

As we started to lose money, ownership meetings took on an entirely new stress level for me. When I had to ask for the first cash call to continue to finance the operation, some investors began talking about how long they wanted to continue. They were reaching a breaking point and that was understandable, even as it added pressure to an already difficult situation.

I felt like the duck on the pond. My head was above water, but my feet were going a hundred miles an hour beneath the surface to stay afloat. The ownership group was not to be dismissed. It represented some of the brightest and most successful and talented people in Western Massachusetts.

The MassMutual insurance company, a corporate giant in Springfield, appointed different representatives to our board to represent them. Each one brought a different perspective to the meetings - but the bottom line at every meeting was they made one thing clear: they did not want to be part-owners of a hockey team.

Peter Picknelly Jr. who was "asked" by his father to get involved, probably deems it the poorest investment he has ever made. When he had to bring a check for his portion of the cash call, he threw it at me and yelled, "No Mas!" the Spanish words for "no more" and famous words supposedly spoken by boxer Roberto Duran when he was getting clobbered by Sugar Ray Leonard.

Duran claims he never actually said that and blamed broadcaster Howard Cosell for spreading the story. But Peter Picknelly sure said it. Who knew Picknelly was a boxing fan?

The flamboyant and articulate Joe Cambi always had my back, and for that I will always be appreciative. Joe was the marketing guru of the group, and he had no problem with spending money.

He once paid for a film crew to fly in from Chicago to shoot this cool commercial on a pond in East Longmeadow. It cost more than our entire advertising budget, but Joe didn't care. The concept was great, but the other owners did not buy into it. Joe thought he would be reimbursed for his investment, but he never got paid a dime.

He never complained, other than to bust my chops a few times.

Lyman Wood was my go-to guy on finances. The first time Bob Oliver (our vice-president of business) and I had to present our budget, we were both quaking in our boots, even though we had gone over it a hundred times. I decided we would meet with Lyman first and if we could answer all his questions, the presentation to the entire group would be smooth sailing.

It only took Lyman two minutes to scrutinize revenues and expenses before the questions started to fly. We were prepared and we handled each one to his satisfaction.

Lyman was one of the first investors to get on board with us in 1994, and over the years, I leaned on him more than anyone else. He was a very direct, no-nonsense kind of guy and I learned a lot from him. At our board meetings, I purposely had him sit in a location where I could look directly at him.

Lyman was all business. He hated being tied up in minutiae. If things started to get off-course, which they did too often, I could look at Lyman and he would give me the signal to get back on track.

There were Don and Judy Bridge, who stayed on with the new group and were simply two of the nicest people I could have had in my corner. They never complained and they always supported my decisions. They were the consummate citizens any city needs, and which are often hard to find - people who were just happy to be a part of something that was good for the city.

They loved hockey, too. I think the losses and our place in the standings every year bothered them more than writing checks.

As the AHL guide and record book will show, we had dismal teams almost every year. Those teams set records for the longest AHL playoff drought by a franchise. The pressure was on me to turn it around, as the fans were in an uproar, and rightfully so. We tried changing affiliations - Phoenix, Los Angeles (which supplied players in a shared agreement for a time), Tampa Bay and Edmonton, but nothing much was working on the ice.

At the box office, it was ugly, as attendance really started to drop off. Inevitably, the ownership group finally decided it had lost enough money, and they came me with the message that I had to sell the team. They were clear that their intentions were to keep the team in Springfield, but if that did not happen, they wanted me to negotiate a deal with the highest bidder.

As I now look back to those days, it was the first time I knew that the pressure I was under was starting to take its toll on my health and at home. I wanted so badly to keep the team in Springfield, but having gone through the ownership change before, I knew the chances of finding a new local ownership group were slim. I was logging 15-hour days, trying to run the franchise as president, and spending almost every other waking minute trying to find investors.

Over several weeks, our lawyer, Mike Sweet and I reviewed 31 different proposals from a variety of individuals and teams. Some are worth mentioning. Others were just tire- kickers who had dreams of owning a hockey franchise but not the wallet to back it up. But some of the interest was serious.

The first solid offer came from the Dallas Stars and their representative, Rick McLaughlin. Dallas wanted an AHL team to put in the new building in Austin, Texas. Obviously, that meant Springfield would lose its franchise.

Rick and I had agreed to terms, but I simply could not pull the trigger and at the last minute, I backed out of the deal. My gut told me there was something else out there. The ownership group was not very happy with me, but they supported my decision.

Even so, the message was sent loudly and clearly: Landon, don't screw this up!

My old friend Ed Anderson (former owner of the Portland and Providence franchise) set up a meeting through a friend of his, Jim Bennett, in Newport, Rhode Island. This sit-down came with a billionaire hedge fund guy out of Chicago who had his own mansion - and certainly a unique way of doing business. After about half an hour of pretty pointless conversation and a couple minutes of inhaling little finger sandwiches his wife had made, he threw an offer at me. It was for two million bucks, and not even close to what we wanted.

I had to make a decision on the spot. There would be no negotiation, nor was I going to be able to make any phone calls. As I wiped the mustard from my face, I politely thanked him for the offer, packed up my briefcase and left.

I met several times with a guy named Steve Ryan who had great connections with people in hockey, particularly with the Pittsburgh Penguins and Philadelphia Flyers. Steve was pretty sure he could broker a deal to get the team sold. He brought a couple of young guys from New Jersey to the table who were big sports fans, knew little about hockey but wanted to own a team.

They'd agreed if we made a deal, they would keep it in Springfield and I could continue to run it. I thought for sure this deal was going to happen. They had the money and had made a good offer. I took it to the ownership group for their approval. It looked like it would happen, but then the Jersey Boys backed out and I never heard from them again.

I even went to my hometown to Kingston, Ontario to meet with a very successful businessman who wanted to buy a professional team. He was in the steel business, loved hockey and at the time owned a Junior B team in Canada.

He had a daughter who was about to graduate from the University of Connecticut, and also a son who was a goalie at Clarkson. His idea was to buy the team, have me stay on and teach his daughter the business after she graduated.

His offer was on the low side, but it was one I thought we'd accept because it meant the team would stay in Springfield. Unfortunately, he became very ill and had to withdraw the offer.

By this time, ownership was really getting frustrated and the pressure on me was reaching a boiling point. I was miserable to be around, and I was taking it out on my family. Then I received a call from Laurence Gilman, who at one time was the assistant general manager of the Phoenix Coyotes, and with whom I had worked closely. Laurence was now working for the Vancouver Canucks and he made the call with his owners and lawyers in the room. I was by myself in my office.

His offer was one that, for all intents and purposes I should have accepted on the spot. He made it clear that the team would leave Springfield. I didn't hesitate. I turned the offer down.

Was I a complete, absolute idiot? Time would tell. I'm not even sure I shared this offer with the ownership group.

There was also Lou Lamoriello, one of the most respected people in professional hockey. He'd had success at the college level, with the New Jersey Devils and then with the Toronto Maple Leafs, who were enjoying some success. He was also involved in a little back-door dealing that could have had the Devils operating their farm team in Springfield.

Lou had heard from his friend, Jim Bennett in Providence, that our franchise was for sale. I got the call and Bob Oliver and I made the trip down to New Jersey to meet with Lou in his office.

He was cordial, though in typical Lamoriello style, there was little small talk. We were in and out of his office in about 15 minutes, but from that first meeting, I had a bad feeling about what was going on.

Lou also stopped in to Springfield for a site visit and expressed how much he liked the facility and our operation. This is where the negotiations got complicated.

During the weeks of trying to find a buyer, we had purposely kept the news away from Springfield Mayor Domenic Sarno, who had always been wonderful to us. The ownership group did not want to alarm Sarno about the possibility of the team leaving Springfield, and since we really had no news, there was not much to tell him. But that all blew up in our faces.

Without our knowledge and certainly without our approval, Bennett made his own visit to Springfield to visit with Mayor Sarno and tell him how he was putting a group together to buy the franchise with the New Jersey Devils as the NHL affiliate. Jim and I had never spoken about a price; in fact, we had not even begun discussions about him purchasing the franchise.

To our view, Jim was simply filling the Mayor with nothing but baloney. The Mayor was very upset, and rightfully so, so we had to parade ourselves in front of him to explain what was going on.

That was as far as this deal went. The ownership group wanted no part of doing business with Bennett. This left me with the job of telling Lamoriello.

When he came to see a game, I met with him outside the press box in the upper level of the MassMutual Center. I think everyone in the building could hear him screaming at me and accusing me of making him think that we had a deal. But the truth is that his own guy had fouled it up and ruined it by going behind our backs.

By now, we were into the 2010 season and the ownership group had had enough. I was given the ultimatum: find a buyer and do it fast. I had been working behind the scenes with a group from Des Moines that had not yet made an offer. After a couple of more calls, they agreed to pay us $3 million, but they made it clear the team would be moving.

At this point, the owners did not care. They had been bleeding financially and were willing to take a big haircut in the pocketbook to get out, if even it meant the team was leaving. Still hoping to find a buyer who would not move the team, I begged them for a little more time and they agreed to give me two weeks - but I was not allowed to let the Des Moines deal fall through the cracks.

By this time, I was a physical and emotional wreck. I had been sleeping three hours a night and actually had my own quiet meltdown one day in my office, bawling like a baby.

The reckoning moment was coming, and I realized that something I had fought so hard for - something that had been such a big part of so many lives and had defined my own post-playing career - was soon to be snatched away from us. It was a business deal, yes, but personally, it was torture.

19
CHARLIE POMPEA YEARS

I had about ten days to go before I would have to ink a deal with the group in Iowa. I was calling everyone I could think of, trying desperately to come up with a last-minute name who might bail us out and keep the team in Springfield. At that critical moment, I got a call from Phil Shuman, our company accountant and my friend, who wanted me to meet with a friend of his for lunch.

I quickly agreed. The friend was Charlie Pompea. A major moment in the history of Springfield hockey, not to mention my own life, was about to take place.

We met at the Canoe Club in Connecticut and I made my pitch. Charlie used to watch the old New Haven Blades and he said he liked hockey but did not want to buy a franchise.

On my way back from the meeting, though, I got a call from him, telling me that if I could get a group together, he would be a part of it. That was nice of him, but I was out of contacts and time... or at least, so I thought.

It was Columbus Day, and we were hosting our annual charity golf tournament that Shuman ran for us. When he put me in a foursome with Charlie, I decided to take a different approach. Never once during the 18 holes did I mention business. I wanted Charlie to enjoy himself and maybe have a couple of adult beverages.

At the final hole, he asked me how I was making out in finding an investor group. I told him I had nothing, I was out of time and it would be announced shortly that the team would be moved.

Following the golf tournament, we had a banquet at Crestview Country Club in Agawam and Phil asked me to speak. I gave a pretty passionate speech about how much the franchise meant to our community. I thought it would be my last opportunity to do so. As people were filing out at the end of the night, Charlie asked me to stay for a beer.

Springfield Falcons left wing Henrik Samuelsson [L] attempts a shot on Albany Devils goalie Ken Appleby during game at the MassMutual Center. Samuelsson had a goal in Springfield's 4-3 overtime victory, Feb. 26, 2016. (Photo by Chris Marion, Courtesy Springfield Falcons).

Providence Bruins goalie Niklas Svedberg gets beat by Springfield Falcons Michael Chaput's shot which tied the game 1-1 in the second period at the MassMutual Center, April 25, 2014. (Photo by Dave Roback, The Republican).

Springfield Falcons President Sarah Pompea announces the Falcons' affiliation with the NHL's Arizona Coyotes at a press conference at the MassMutual Center. At left is Falcons Director of Hockey Operations Bruce Landon, who negotiated the deal, April 17, 2015. (Photo by Kevin Dillon, Republican/MassLive.com).

Huddling over beers in the corner of the room, Charlie and I started working on a deal I could present to my partners.

Charlie's plan was for me to remain as president and also retain a small ownership percentage. The offer was less than Des Moines, Vancouver or Dallas had offered, but the big difference was that the team would remain in Springfield. Our ownership group remained loyal to the city of Springfield and - with some reluctance - agreed to accept the offer.

It was December in 2010 and this was the start of the Charlie Pompea reign, which for me would prove to be bittersweet. I had pulled another rabbit out of my hat at the last minute and, against the odds, had kept the team in Springfield.

Little did I know this rabbit wasn't all warm and fuzzy.

I had what could be best described as a love-hate relationship with Charlie. Some things just drove me crazy.

When Charlie would come into my office, he'd invariably say, "Bruce, this isn't a hobby, it's a business." For someone like myself to hear that after putting my life's sweat and savings into the operation - it was just impossible to swallow.

To this day, I respect that Charlie was willing to put his wallet on the line to keep the team in a city that he was not really invested in. However, as local history will show, he was also a shrewd businessman, and he could be incredibly stubborn once his mind was made up.

Charlie Pompea, left, the new owner of the Springfield Falcons and Bruce Landon, President and General Manager of the Falcons talk with the press prior to the Falcons' game against Connecticut, Jan. 22, 2011. (Photo by David Molnar, The Republican).

It should have been clear to me from the beginning that although we had some things in common, one of them was not how to run a professional hockey team. He'd made his money in the steel business, and from all accounts, he'd run it with an iron fist. That's just not my style and eventually, it wore me out.

I was too old and too stubborn to change my style, and he began forcing me to make decisions that were changing me as a person.

One of Charlie's ideas was to force myself and the staff to wear red, white and blue clothes to every game. Our "uniform" was to consist of a blue blazer with either a white shirt or blue shirt and a red or navy-blue tie. More than once, my staff came to me complaining that they were embarrassed and were even taking some ribbing from a few of the fans.

I tried to speak to Charlie about it, but it was a waste of time. Like just about everything else, he would not budge once he had made a decision. The word "compromise" was not in his personal dictionary.

One night, we were driving to Boston together for a meeting and the song "The Bird is the Word" came on the radio. This was an early 1960s song that a group called the Rivingtons had created and was made famous in a different version by another band called the Trashmen. (The second version actually reached No. 4 on the pop charts.)

Well, it was a No. 1 hit with Charlie, who started dancing in his seat to the song

Springfield Falcon Team Owner Charlie Pompea (left) shakes the hand of General Manager Bruce Landon as he was addressing fans and media on Feb. 10, 2013 at the MassMutual Center to announce the new Springfield Falcon Charitable Foundation to enrich the lives of children and families throughout Greater Springfield to be led by his daughter Sarah. (Photo by Michael Beswick, The Republican).

and proclaimed it would be our new theme song. I had no problem with the choice of a song, but Charlie demanded it be played three times every game - regardless of what else was going on during the game.

Charlie spent most of the winters in Jupiter, Florida. He watched most of the games on the AHL telecast. I can't even recall the number of times he would call me during the third period and scream at me because he'd heard his favorite song only twice during the game. The calls during the third period also came when the team was not playing well.

Charlie's reaction would be to tear into me because he felt our coach should have been yelling more at the players. He'd also send me a text message during the game and yell at me because he had "seen" one of the employees on the concourse who was not wearing red, white and blue.

Of course, there was no way he could have seen someone on the concourse, not while he was sitting on his lazyboy in Florida watching the game on a computer monitor. But someone else could. His daughter, Sarah, would be in the house and she reported back to him on everything.

I had a file full of emails from Charlie, and some of them were biting and hurtful. There were times I wanted to tell him to go jump in the lake (or do something worse) and walk out the door, but that was not my style.

So, I kept reminding myself that it was his money, he was paying me a decent salary and, as an owner, he had the right to do what he wanted. I had to find a way to rise above it.

That wasn't easy. Even though I was the contact with our NHL partner and had the respect of all the NHL clubs with whom I had ever worked, Charlie never wanted me to watch the games. It didn't matter that I would get a call from the NHL general manager or assistant GM after a game to ask about a certain player or how the game had gone. Charlie always wanted me in the stands, talking to the fans, and he refused to allow me to go to the press box.

I got in the habit of hiding from Charlie and his daughter by finding a spot high up in the corner of the building, lurking in the darkness behind a curtain. It was pretty sad, but it was the only way I could see what was going on down on the ice.

Charlie's idea of my job was the opposite of what I'd always done. From the first day I'd retired and gone to the front office, I'd made a habit of interacting with fans at the games. I followed the same routine for over 40 years.

I'd always gone to the press room early to say hello to the media and joke around with the off-ice officials, who were all volunteers. I wanted them to always know how much I appreciated what they did for us. Then I'd go to the concourse and make several rounds talking to fans, listening to their complaints or sometimes, their compliments. I would talk to the concession vendors and the security guards and make notes on everything.

It was during one of these walks I caught one of the long-time employees of the building letting fans in for free. He was fired the next day. Over the years, some of the other things that happened during these walks were priceless.

I once had an elderly lady grab me by the ear and drag me into the arena. She pointed up to the ceiling and said the light was shining in her eyes. I offered to get her a pair of sunglasses. Unfortunately, she had no sense of humor. The next day I had the building change the direction of the light. I tried to pay attention to all the little things.

One night as I was making my rounds, a fan who had to weigh in at about 300 pounds approached me holding three hot dogs. He got in my face, inhaled one of the dogs with one bite, then spit it out in front of me and roared, "this is the worse (bleeping) hot dog I have ever eaten."

We did not control the concessions, but I wanted to make him happy and asked him what I could do for him. He told me to buy him some nachos, which I did. As he walked away, he was still holding two hot dogs and balancing a full plate of nachos. Just for laughs, I decided to follow him.

He went up to his seat and devoured two of the "worst" hot dogs he'd ever had, then went to work on the nachos. He saw me out of the corner of his eye, reached down and grabbed his beer, and raised it in a toast as if he were saying "thanks, sucker" for the free nachos.

All of this meant nothing to Charlie, who demanded I work the crowd during the game. The problem was that fans come to the game to enjoy the action, not

Bob Oliver, Senior Vice President of the Springfield Falcons' Organization, right, presents Holyoke's Brian Rokowski with the Rob Murray Award at the High School Hockey Banquet at the Dante Club in West Springfield, May 1, 2011. (Photo By David Molnar, The Republican).

Bruce Landon announced he was stepping down as president, general manager and minority owner during a press conference on Feb. 24, 2014. Here he gets a hug from Charlie Pompea. (Photo by Dave Roback, The Republican).

to have me in their ear while the play is going on. But just to please him, I would come down from my hiding place a couple of times during the game and sit with some friends in the stands.

With all of this going on, I was starting to get very resentful at the way I was being treated. I finally said "the hell with it" on the blue blazer, white shirt and red tie, and started dressing how I wanted. I figured I was over 60 and I had earned that right.

Charlie always accused me of being too soft on my employees, which probably angered me more than anything else during the entire time I worked for him. His style was so different that I came to believe he had no clue as to why I operated the way I did - and why it worked. I treated those who worked for me with respect, and I knew that most of them would have gone through a brick wall for me or do anything needed to be done to help the franchise.

I got to know each one of them on a personal level. I always understood they had families and had to deal with their own personal problems. They did not make much money and they worked crazy hours, but Charlie seemed oblivious to all this.

If someone showed up ten minutes late and he found out about it - which he always seemed to do - he would go off on me. It didn't matter that I had given that employee permission to be late, knowing they would work well into the early part of the night.

During my entire career in management, there were only a handful of times I had to discipline someone or fire an employee, and it was always due to lack of performance. On more than one occasion, Charlie made me convinced he simply had no "feel" for our business or for the people who worked in this industry.

One example came with Bob Oliver, who was our first hire back in 1994, and who had remained on as my right-hand guy through all of the years and ownership changes. Bob was our vice-president of business and you could not find a more loyal, hardworking, high-integrity guy. He never looked at the clock, and it was not unusual for him to work well past midnight.

Bob took pride in his job and in the franchise, but he became Charlie's personal whipping boy. One example: Charlie demanded his financial reports be emailed to him at 4 pm on Fridays. It didn't matter what else Bob had on his plate - if Charlie did not get his reports before 4 pm., I would get the call.

I understood the need for Charlie to see his financials, but I also knew that Bob was being pulled in different directions at times. I could not see what difference it made if he was a half hour late. But Charlie was the boss and I was getting tired of being chewed out, so I had to demand Bob be on time no matter what the situation.

Over the years, the anger and resentment over how I was being treated, and how I was being forced to treat the employees, began taking its toll on me. I could see the breaking point coming where I would either have a heart attack or a nervous breakdown. Finally, it was over another "issue" with Bob, one that convinced me I could never be comfortable working with Charlie.

Bob had come to see me about playing in a Tuesday night golf league. This meant that on Tuesdays, he would leave the office at 4:30 rather than 5 pm. As mentioned, Bob was a workaholic for me, working most weekends and weekend nights in the fall and winter, in addition to the hours he put in during the day.

That was what the job demanded. I can never remember him calling in sick, and he was always in the office early. So, it was not a big deal to me for Bob to play golf late on a Tuesday afternoon and I thought it would be good for him.

Charlie went nuts. Not only did he overrule me and say there was no way Bob could leave early to golf, he thought I was an idiot and too soft by allowing him to do so.

I think that was the final straw for Bob. He realized his time with Charlie was coming to an end, but it was a question of who was going to go first, him or me.

Most people in Springfield probably assumed the Falcons were a financially losing proposition, but with the final sale of the franchise, Charlie did not lose money in Springfield. To his credit, in the one year he made a nice profit, he did give the employees - and myself - a nice bonus.

Charlie did have a generous side to him. When he did attend games he was always buying hats and passing them out to the kids in the stands.

In this regard, he came across as good-time Charlie, but I was dealing with the other side of him. I was starting to crack under the pressure, and the final blow was about to come.

I had arrived home after a home game around midnight. We had won the game in front of a large and noisy crowd, I was in a great mood and poured myself a stiff Scotch to cap off the evening when the email came in on my phone.

I sat there in complete shock as I read a very, very long negative message from him where he ripped me, the staff and everything else he could think of. I started to shake, felt like I was going to throw up and hurled my phone across the room. My wife thought I was having a heart attack and she wanted to call 911.

I gave her the phone to read the email and after about two minutes, she started to cry. She wanted to know how often this happened and I told her I had a file full of them. It was in my living room at midnight on that Saturday that she told me I didn't deserve to be treated this way, and it was time to put an end to it.

That was all I had to hear. I was a beaten man and was very worried about my health. I called Charlie and set up a face-to-face meeting with him. I told him I wanted to step down as president, but I would remain to oversee the hockey operations part of the job. After all the years, I told him, the day-to-day grind was affecting my health. I did not have the nerve to tell him that he had put me over the edge.

I honestly believe that deep down, he was happy. I felt his plan all along had been for his daughter to be in charge. This just made it a lot easier.

Charlie held a press conference to deliver the news and in typical Charlie fashion, he praised me as if I were a saint. He spoke about what a great job I had done over the years, and that it was time for me to spend more time with my family. He also said he would begin the search immediately for a new president, which he did.

His new hire did not last long, and he had Sarah, his daughter, fire him. Charlie called me and asked me if I would sit in with her when she had to give the fired executive the news, because he was afraid of what the guy might do.

Within days, Sarah became the new president of the Springfield Falcons. That's when things really got interesting. Sarah is a wonderful young lady and I had recommended to Charlie that we hire her for a marketing position, which we did, even though she had very, very limited experience. However, to give her the title of president was not fair to her or to anyone else on the staff. Everyone resented her, and she never was able to gain the respect of the employees because they knew her dad was calling the shots.

All the crazy rules that Charlie put in place, like the dress code, went right out the window when Sarah took over. As for interacting with the fans, no one really got to know her, because she would spend most of the time hiding in her office during games.

Sarah was in over her head, and I felt sorry for her. There were certainly many things she could do well in life but taking over as president of a hockey team that was one step below the NHL is not something everyone can just walk in and do, and she couldn't, either.

More than once, Charlie asked me to watch out for her so she wouldn't fail. I tried, but when she started showing up late almost every day and often simply disappearing for hours during the day, I lost interest.

Charlie is a bright man and I think he realized that Sarah was just not cut out for the job. However, it was his daughter and I think deep down, he knew the only way out was to sell the franchise, rather than admit his decision to put her in charge was a complete bust.

During this time, I was heavily involved in negotiations with the Arizona Coyotes to sign a long-term affiliation agreement. I was dealing exclusively with their Don Maloney, their general manager, and like most of these discussions, it was give-and-take for both parties.

I was trying to get the best financial arrangement possible for us. Controlling affiliation fees is the only way a franchise like Springfield has a chance to survive. We had reached an agreement on a deal, or at least I thought we had, when I was at the bar at Springfield Country Club enjoying dinner with my wife and I received a call from Don.

He said his owners would not sign the agreement unless I put a clause in the contract that gave them the right to purchase the franchise if we were going to sell. I did not like this on-the-spot, last-minute surprise and told as much to Don. However, I told him I would call Charlie and get back to him.

I remember that conversation with him like it was yesterday. I told Charlie we should not agree to it, as it would limit Charlie's bargaining power in the event that someday he did want to sell the franchise. He agreed with me.

I told him I would call Don back and tell him we would not agree to it. We would agree to a clause that said in the event we wanted to sell, we would give them the opportunity, but that we could sell it to anyone we wanted.

The deal reached agreement. Little did I know at the time that it would come back and haunt both me and the city of Springfield.

Charlie did have his generous side; he lent support, for instance, when Springfield was devastated by a tornado in 2010. But personally, he had no ties to Springfield and to make it worse, his daughter did not like playing the role of president and didn't like what she was doing. I'd always had the sense that Charlie might at some time decide to pull the plug, but I never expected him to do it behind my back.

I was naive in thinking that if he was going to sell, he would come to me and give me a chance, like everyone else had done, to try and find a buyer to keep it in Springfield. That's not what happened, though.

Normally, Charlie would tell me when he was coming. When he showed up at my office unannounced one day, I knew something was up.

Sarah was a ghost and nowhere to be seen. Charlie walked into my office and told me he had sold the franchise. I was not shocked about that, but when he told me he had sold it to Arizona and they would be moving it out of Springfield, I was livid.

Without giving it a thought, he had just wiped away many, many years of hockey in Springfield without an iota of concern for the fans, me or anyone else. When I finally gained my composure, I asked him, why Arizona?

His answer made no sense. He said that our affiliation agreement stated he had to sell to them. I tried to argue with him that he was wrong, and that all we had to do was give them a chance to make an offer, but that we could negotiate with others as well.

He really didn't care what I thought. I was told to keep it quiet because he was still finalizing the deal. I kept it from everyone, including my own family, but down deep, I wanted to go public and blast him to the limits for what he was doing.

But that simply was not my style. He gave me a hug and walked out of the office. A week later he showed up again in my office, and this is when things really exploded.

Charlie came flying into my office and he was fuming. He accused me of sabotaging his deal to buy the Portland Pirates. Nothing could have been further from the truth. I had asked Charlie for permission to talk to AHL president Dave Andrews, simply to find out if there was the possibility of another franchise that may want to relocate to Springfield.

Charlie had given me permission to do so. Dave told me the Portland franchise was for sale. It is interesting because during my conversation with Charlie, he told me that if I wanted to buy Portland, to go ahead and do so. I told him right to his face that I did not have the money to make that happen.

On the advice of Dave Andrews, I made one call to Florida Panthers' executive Eric Joyce to find out the particulars of their affiliation agreement with Portland. In our industry, this is not uncommon as we share this type of information all the time.

I also had received a call from Lyman Bullard, the governor of the Portland franchise and someone I had really respected over the years.

He asked me one question: when was my group going to put an offer in to buy Portland? I wish I had this conversation on tape. I told him I was not part of a group, but if there was a group, they would have to act soon because the league spring meetings were coming up. That was the end of the conversation and it was 100 percent true.

I can't validate this, but I've always wondered if Charlie was getting some bad information about my involvement from someone in Portland. In his mind, I became the bad guy.

After the visit to my office where he told me he was selling the team to Arizona, he told me he would pay me through the end of May and pay my health insurance. A week later, that deal was off the table.

He told me my health insurance would be ending. I could keep my phone, but I would have to start making the payments. Then he walked out the door. No hug this time around.

Within 10 minutes, my computer was shut down and I lost all the contacts I had built up over many, many years. Despite all of this, I never said one negative word about Charlie to the media. I took my standard position that as an owner, he had the right to do what he wanted to do, even if it meant selling the franchise and knowing it would be moving.

I should be carrying a grudge about all of this, but I've worked hard to condition myself not to do so. It probably cost me a lot of money, but I did not have the fight left in me to go after him for what I believed he owed me. His reasons for dismissing me were totally wrong and, for lack of any other reason to believe them, I have assumed he was basing them on false information he had received from someone or somewhere.

But for all the pressures and problems of those years, there's one fact I would never deny. When no one else would step up in 2010 to keep hockey in Springfield, Charlie Pompea did. And for that, I am grateful.

20
COACHES

Over my long history in hockey, both in my amateur and professional days, I have either played for, or been involved with, many coaches. Some have had great careers. Others should have taken up another line of work.

I choose not to reflect on their coaching abilities as many of them simply were not given the tools to succeed. However, many of them have stories worth telling for different reasons.

Some had great one-liners you simply can't forget.

Don Blackburn coached the Whalers briefly, and I had the chance to play for Blackie. He was inexperienced as a coach when he went behind the bench for the 1975-76 season, but he could crack up a room quickly.

In one game, he was furious because we were being out-hit and our players showed no signs of wanting to get involved physically. At the end of the first period, Blackie ripped into the guys.

"Their forwards could have a dozen eggs in their pants and stand in front of the net and at the end of the game, not one (expletive deleted) egg would be broken," he told them. The guys got the message because when the next period began, we started whacking guys all over the place and ended up having a major brawl.

During another game, I was on the bench and not playing. One of our younger guys skated over and started whining that he was being targeted by their tough guy. Blackie told him to stuff his stick in his mouth and see how much he liked being a beaver.

Jimmy Roberts was a great coach and a no-nonsense kind of guy. One day I was in his office, when he was talking about one of his players, Jimmy said, "Brucie, I love him like a son, but I hate him as a hockey player."

Above: From left, Jack Butterfield, Chairman AHL, Falcons coach Paul Gillis, Terry McDonnell, Vice President of Operations for the Hartford Whalers, and Falcons President Bruce Landon, July 29, 1994. (Republican file photo).

Left: Gary Dineen, center of the Junior Whalers Hockey team with Doug Janik of Agawam (l), and Dan Cavanaugh of Springfield (r) at a practice at the Enfield Twin Rinks, Mar. 11, 1997. (Photo by Mark M. Murray, The Republican).

On another time, he was sitting in his office with me and he received a call from Bill Torrey, the general manager of the New York Islanders. Bill told him he was sending down one of their young prospects. Jimmy hung up the phone and relayed the conversation to me.

"Prospects, my (butt). They are coach killers. They (stink) and the coach gets fired," he said.

On another occasion when they sent him a player, Jimmy said, "Brucie, I can't make a concert violinist out of the banjo player they sent me."

We have had teams in Springfield that were so bad with low talent that the legendary Scotty Bowman could not have milked more wins out of them. It was unfortunate, but the coach sometimes took the blame, far more than was fair.

Bruce Boudreau. (The Republican file photo).

One example came after Tom Webster was hired by George Leary to coach the Indians. We were affiliated with the New York Rangers and Herb Brooks - fresh off his Miracle on Ice with the 1980 gold-medal U.S. hockey team the previous year - was coaching the Rangers. Craig Patrick was the GM.

Webbie was a former teammate of mine. During my playing days, I always thought he would make a good coach.

In New York, the Rangers were loaded with many European players and Brooks had them playing a creative offensive style. They became famous, in fact, for the weave play, and Patrick wanted Webster to make sure that the guys in Springfield were playing the same system.

Springfield Indians 1984-1985 Coach Lorne Henning, Oct. 11, 1984. (Photo by Dave Roback, The Republican).

    This happens far too many times. I think sometimes the NHL general managers forget the talent level is not the same in the AHL. But Webster wanted to obey orders, so he tried to get his players to play the same way.

    In one game, our players came out of the defensive zone with the puck and tried the famous weave play as they went through center ice. The only problem was they ran over each other in the neutral zone and looked more like the Keystone Cops than an attacking hockey team.

    The other team picked up the puck, walked in and scored. I was sitting next to owner George Leary and I thought he was going into cardiac arrest.

Springfield Indians Coach John Wilson. (Photo by Don Fontaine, The Republican).

I felt badly for Tom, but you need to play the cards you are dealt. Despite the dismal year in Springfield, Webster went on to a successful coaching career. My guess is that he never tried the weave play again.

I made it a habit of never socializing too much with coaches once the season would start. It was a tough balancing act for me because I really liked the guys and their families, but I did not want to get caught in an awkward situation.

In the early years, I would often get a call from the NHL general manager to get my opinion on how the coach was doing. I did not want to be a hypocrite and be out for dinner and drinking with a coach one night, then telling his boss the next day that I thought he was a lousy coach.

Bruce Landon [far left] and Pete Stemkowski (2nd from right). (Photo courtesy Landon Family).

In the off-season, when the coaches got settled into the area, it was different. I enjoyed golfing with the guys or just hanging out with them.

Marc Potvin was one of the Springfield coaches whose company I really enjoyed. He was just a good guy and fun to be around. Like most guys who had to play the tough-guy role in their playing days, Marc was just the opposite away from the rink. He was very intense, but he could enjoy a good laugh and share a good story.

I remember (with a hint of embarrassment) the day my wife and I invited Potsy, his wife, Maria, and their two young kids over to our house for a barbecue. We were having a great time until I had to fire up the grill. The problem was that I had no propane.

Potsy just laughed and busted my balls that the oversight was intentional. We packed up all the food and went over to his house, where he took over the cooking duties.

Every once in a while in the afternoon we would slip over to Collins Tavern, a great watering hole in West Springfield. Over a couple of beers, we would just shoot the breeze about families, hockey or whatever the hot topic was at the time. But losing was taking its toll on Marc, and you could see it in his eyes and his body language.

He was a very competitive person, and I think he had a lot of trouble leaving the game at the rink. He coached us for two years and although we never made the playoffs in those two years, he made a nice impression on everyone he touched in Springfield as a coach.

The one exception might be the man who pushed Marc's wrong buttons during a men's hockey league game.

In addition to being a very physical forward, Marc was also a pretty decent player. During the men's league games, he would just take it easy and enjoy working up a good sweat. But one young guy thought he was pretty tough and kept taking liberties with Potsy by slashing him or being too rough.

Disregarding several warnings to stop, the guy not only persisted but made the mistake of dropping his gloves and challenging Marc to a fight. All it took was one punch and Potvin knocked the guy out cold.

You poke the bear once too often, and you pay the price.

I was devastated when I heard Marc had taken his own life while on a road trip for the Adirondack Frostbite, which he was coaching in the ECHL after his time in Springfield. I have no idea whether it was the pressure of the game or other demons he battled, and it is not my place to try and speculate. All I know is we lost a really good guy, way too young.

Guys like Marty McSorley and Kelly Buckberger are super-good guys and were well-established as NHL players before they retired. McSorley was well-known as Wayne Gretzky's "protector," but he also built a reputation as not just a tough guy but one who could play. Gretzky said every team needed a guy like McSorley.

McSorley and Buckberger had limited success as coaches, although Marty got us into the playoffs in his first year as coach, despite our having a losing record. We lost in Round 1, but for many years, even making the playoffs in Springfield was a bonus, no matter how you got there.

Marty's coaching career lasted only two seasons in Springfield. Bucky had a .500 record, but we failed to make the playoffs. He went on to a long tenure as an assistant NHL coach in Edmonton.

Paul Gillis was our first coach with the Falcons. Like Bucky and McSorley and some other guys, he was not prepared for the AHL at the time and was put in a position to fail, primarily because these guys were not given nearly enough talent.

The Edmonton Oilers never provided the players we needed to be successful, and good people like Jeff Truitt and Rob Daum paid the price. Jeff was hired as an assistant for us after a long and successful coaching career in Western Canada. He was later promoted to head coach but wound up getting fired.

It was not because of his lack of coaching ability. He was trying to make filet mignon out of leftover cold cuts. Jeff was a stand-up guy and we were known to throw back a few adult beverages a couple of times during his short time in Springfield.

Rob Daum also failed in Springfield, despite having had success in both the Western Hockey League and at Houston of the AHL.

Having no talent or very limited talent and being expected to win in a league as strong as the AHL is almost impossible.

For my money, the AHL is too tough a league to take a player who has just retired and put him in charge of a team. The first step should be to allow newly retired
players to learn the game at the AHL level by making them an assistant, with an experienced head coach from whom they can learn.

Brad Larsen, one of my personal favorite guys to come through Springfield, was handled the right way. Larsen spent his last year as a player in Portland of the AHL, but he was given some coaching responsibilities. He was then hired as an assistant under Rob Riley, who received the head coaching job in Springfield after a long and successful college coaching career.

Rob is a great student of the game and a wonderful teacher. His lack of success had nothing to do with his knowledge of the game or coaching abilities, but simply because he was given a horrible team in both of years.

It gave Brad Larsen the chance to experience first-hand how tough the AHL is, and what it takes to be a good coach. When I received a call from the Columbus Blue Jackets, asking if I thought Larsen was ready for the head coaching job, there was no hesitation on my part whatsoever.

He was a guy who had carved out a career as a solid NHL player through hard work and discipline. He had three years to hone his coaching craft and I thought the players would play hard for him. As head coach of the Falcons, he had two successful years and made the playoffs both years.

Brad was, and is, one of the most complete professionals from a coaching perspective I've had the chance to around. I may be biased here because "Lars" really let me be a part of the hockey side of the business. He would ask and value my opinion, and that meant a lot to me.

Although he can talk a dog off a meat wagon, he wanted input from others and listened to what you had to say. I also loved the fact that he was a devoted family man and knew his priorities in life.

We used to enjoy a good time after the games as well but only if we'd won or picked up a point. Like most coaches, Brad enjoyed a cold beer after a game and it was always more satisfying if the team had won.

Socializing and hockey can mix if winning is always the priority. For the most part, I am a Scotch drinker. My wife, Marcia, went out and had a couple of glasses made - one for me and the other for Brad.

Springfield Falcons' Head Coach Brad Larsen watches the action between his team and the Manchester Monarchs at the MassMutual Center in 2012.
(Photo by David Molnar, The Republican).

On the glasses were two lines drawn. The line closer to the bottom said one point. The other line, closer to the top, said two points.

Once, I brought in a bottle of Johnny Walker Blue, which is top-shelf and very expensive. After each win or even if we just picked up one point, while Brad was in addressing the team, I would be in pouring the Scotch. Larsen hated Scotch, but he knew how much I enjoyed it, so he would force himself to drink it as we toasted the team's accomplishments.

Assistant coach Jared Bednar soon joined in for the post-game celebration. On many nights, Columbus assistant general manager Chris MacFarland would be in town, so we couldn't leave him out.

My Johnny Walker Blue at $200 a bottle, did not last long. We had a pretty good home record, so my Scotch bill was probably a thousand bucks, but worth every penny.

It did not surprise me when Columbus promoted Brad to be the assistant coach in Columbus. He'd been patient and had paid his dues. I knew then that he had the makings of being a very successful head coach in the National Hockey League, if that's what he would so choose to pursue.

We had a few coaches who had classic Jekyll-and-Hyde personalities, and I was amazed at how drastically they could change. Dirk Graham was one.

Graham who had coached part of one year in Chicago was named by Tampa Bay to be our head coach in 2004. I'd played golf with Dirk a couple of times in the off-season and really enjoyed his company. But when the season started, he became a totally different person.

We had a god-awful team and maybe that was why he took out his frustrations on everyone around him. He was miserable all the time and could not get along with anyone. He yelled at the guys who ran the building and he was never happy with the ice conditions.

Of all the coaches we ever had in Springfield, he's the only one where I had the arena building operations manager call me and warn me that if Dirk did not respect his staff better, they were going to refuse to bring out the Zamboni.

One Saturday morning, our team dentist wanted to drop off some supplies he was donating to the team. He walked in to the trainer's office and because he was wearing jeans, Dirk completely went off on him, almost physically throwing him out of the room. The next day, the dentist called me and said he has never been so embarrassed in his life - and he quit on the spot.

Dirk only coached two years in Springfield, missing the playoffs each year, and he never coached after that. He went on to become an excellent pro scout and I am happy that he found his hockey niche.

To this day, I think that if the Dirk I knew in the summer could have been the same guy during the season, he would have had much more success.

During my long playing career, every coach brought a different skill set to their role behind the bench. There have been too many coaches for me to talk about all of them and what they had to offer. Gary Dineen, who was George Leary's hire to coach the Indians, was light years ahead of his time in the way he thought about the game.

When Gary was fired, he soured on the pro game and turned his talents to developing some of the best amateur players to come out of this area. There is no doubt that had Gary been able to move forward with a professional coaching career, and chosen to do so, he could have been a good one.

The NHL wants and needs to use the AHL as a developmental league. More and more of the coaches being hired have to be good teachers as well.

Tampa Bay hired Steve Stirling to coach us for two years and although we did not have success on the ice, Steve was a great teacher for the young players. He had earned his coaching stripes with a successful college coaching career. After he left Springfield, he was a head coach for three more seasons, first in Norfolk and then in Germany and Italy, until he made the decision that he wanted to finish his career as an assistant.

Ottawa hired him, and he spent seven years with the Binghamton Senators, working with their young prospects before becoming a scout.

Is it just me, or does it seem like we had too many coaches who got their start in Springfield, but just never seemed to turn it into a long career? Gordie Lane was an assistant with the Indians for two years before being given the head job, where he failed miserably. Gordie never coached after that.

He was another victim of bad personnel, perhaps, or maybe he was just not cut out to be a coach.

Peter Stemkowski was a midseason replacement hired by George Leary, and he only coached that one year. Peter had had a long and distinguished career as a player (and became known, among other things, for being one of the game's best faceoff men), but maybe the small taste of being in charge behind the bench was enough for him.

John Hanna was also hired by Leary for the start of the 1976-77 season, but he was involved in a bad accident which may have hurt his coaching career. Other than two games in the United States Hockey League, a full 10 years after he left Springfield, he never coached again.

Orland Kurtenbach was hired to coach the Indians in 1982 after having some experience as an NHL head coach in Vancouver, and three years in the Central Hockey League. We did not the make playoffs and his pro coaching career came to a screeching halt.

Owner Eddie Shore poses with standout members of his 1961-62 American Hockey League and Calder Cup championship team. From left: Jimmy Anderson, Bill McCreary, Floyd Smith, Bruce Cline, Brian Kilrea, Shore, and Bill Sweeney. (Republican file photo).

With all the failures, there have been some former coaches we saw behind the bench in Springfield who did go on to long careers. Bob Berry was a mid-season replacement in Springfield during the 1977-78 after hanging up his skates, and only coached us for 23 games, but that started him on a coaching career that would last almost 20 seasons.

Lorne Henning, one of Peter Cooney's favorite coaches, came to us from the Islanders after having served as their assistant for three years. Lorne had a losing record with only 36 wins in 80 games, but it did get us into the playoffs, where he lost in the first round.

Henning went on to Coach for another 16 seasons as either a head or assistant coach in the NHL.

One of the more successful, but for some reason less heralded coaches we had in Springfield was Kevin McCarthy. After cutting his teeth as a coach in Hershey and then as an assistant with the Whalers, he was hired to be our head coach for the 1995 season.

"Kato" had instant success. He guided the team to back-to- back playoff appearances, then went on to become an outstanding assistant coach with the Carolina Hurricanes, Philadelphia Flyers and - still going strong more than 20 years after Springfield - the Nashville Predators.

Dave Farrish was behind the bench for three years with the Falcons, starting in 1997 after having some success in Moncton of the AHL. Farrish also had limited success in the IHL with the Fort Wayne Komets.

Farrish coached our team to the playoffs in three straight seasons but lost in the first round every year. He was known to throw pretty good temper tantrums behind the bench, but according to him, nothing like he did in Fort Wayne.

After being disgusted with the officiating one night, he started throwing sticks on to the ice. After that he started removing his sports jacket, tie and shirt before the referee was able to get him kicked out of the game.

"If I am going to get screwed, I might as well take off my clothes," he told the ref.

Dave went to the ECHL for five years with the Louisiana Ice Gators and made the playoffs every year. He finally landed a great gig in Anaheim as an assistant and later did the same with the Toronto Maple Leafs and the Colorado Avalanche.

Coaching at the AHL level is never easy. You are dealing with young prospects, some older guys who still think they should be in the NHL and the "tweeners," - guys good enough to be decent players at the AHL level and able to put up good numbers every year, but somehow just not good enough to make it to the big time.

You are dealing with the egos and sometimes doing the baby-sitting that goes along with having first-round draft picks in your lineup. You're dealing with the long faces and pouting of the guys who just got sent down.

Fans don't realize that coaching decisions are often not made by the coach, but on orders from their boss in the NHL. The NHL boss will demand certain players get opportunities to play on the power play, penalty kill, or at crucial times in the games, sometimes when their play has not justified it.

Fred Creighton coached the Indians for parts of three seasons, beginning in 1985. Creighton had briefly turned his back on the game after the 1979-80 season.

Fred had the Bruins in first place with only 8 games remaining in the regular season and had a remarkable record of 40-23-13. He was called in to GM Harry Sinden's office thinking he was getting a contract extension or maybe a raise. Instead Harry fired him. The reasoning was that Sinden did not think Fred would take them far in the playoffs.

It drove Fred completely out of the game for a short while and in to the men's clothing business. Fred told me the firing and the way it happened was the most humiliating thing that had ever happened to him in his professional career.

Coaching can be a cruel business and sometimes only the strong survive.

21
CHARACTERS IN HOCKEY

With almost 50 years in professional hockey, I had the chance to meet some great and some not-so-great people, but the second types are few and far between. You meet many colorful characters of the game and you simply can't write a book about hockey, especially in Springfield without talking about some of these guys.

There are several that stand out for me and for different reasons. There are names fans will recognize and some they may not, but the stories in some cases are legendary.

The stories about the one and only Eddie Shore are endless, and some are almost too hard to believe. I was involved in a couple of my own personal and true encounters with Mr. Shore at the beginning of my career.

In my very first year as a 20-year-old rookie for the Kings, we had just finished practice when coach Johnny Wilson told me the "old man" wanted to see me back on the ice. I must admit that at the time, all I knew about him was that he was an old hockey player who was running the Eastern States Coliseum where we played.

Eddie was wearing his boots and fedora hat, as always. I was in full goalie gear and going back to the goal. I had no clue what I was in for. All I knew is I wanted to get the hell off the ice and join the guys for a beer at the old Elbow Lounge.

We ended up spending about 45 minutes with Shore standing behind the net, shouting at me on how to move and how to stand. At the time, it made no sense at all, but I had to satisfy both Shore and Wilson.

Finally, Shore walked around in front of me. He stuck a finger the size of a banana in my face and said, "Son, you will never be a goaltender until you learn how to tap dance."

Those were the only words ever exchanged between myself and hockey legend

The longtime equipment manager for the Springfield Falcons hockey team, Ralph Calvanese. (Photo by Don Treeger, The Republican).

Eddie Shore, one of the greatest defensemen in the history of the NHL - a man many call the unquestionably greatest to play his entire career before 1960 - and the dominant figure in Springfield coaching and ownership for 40 years after he played.

In hindsight, maybe I should have checked the yellow pages for the closest dance studio. That wasn't my only episode with Shore, though.

In my rookie season, I took my signing bonus and bought a brand new 'Cuda Convertible. It was white with a red top and nice blue pinstripe that ran up the side. It was my first new car, and I treated it like it was my first newborn baby.

A couple of days after buying the car, we were heading out on a long road trip and I had no idea where to leave my car for the two weeks we were gone. Veteran Randy Miller sat next to me, so I asked him where to park it and he told me where I should leave it.

At the time, it did not dawn on me that mine was the only car there, and that this might be a problem, but I didn't know any better. I got on the bus and headed out of town. When we were gone, Springfield was hit with a major snow and ice storm. When we returned from the trip, it was well after midnight and still snowing.

I went to where my car was supposed to be and all I could see was the tip of the radio antenna sticking out of the snow. I had parked in Shore's parking spot, and rather than having me towed, he just had the plow bury my brand-new car.

I learned two lessons. One was where to park my car. The other was never to listen to Randy Miller.

I should have known better than to take advice from him. He was the same guy I watched on my first day in the dressing room, smothering his body with a very hot liniment of some kind. When I asked him why, he said it was because of the Korean War injuries he had suffered.

Randy was 10 when the Korean War started and 13 when it ended. But what did I know about the Korean War or when it was fought? So, I believed him.

Over the years, I became good friends with Eddie Shore's son, Ted, and heard about all the wonderful things Eddie Shore did for the kids in the area. Most people only remember the crazy stuff, and most of those stories are fabricated. He was a great teacher of the game of hockey, and even though some of his ideas may have seemed radical, he produced results.

Later in my career, when I had success in keeping hockey in Springfield, many people started to throw accolades my way, which still humble me. However, when they started referring me as Mr. Hockey, I was totally embarrassed.

I knew, as I hope everyone in Springfield realizes, that there was and only will be one Mr. Hockey in Springfield, and that was Eddie Shore.

In my first year, we had a rugged defenseman named Roger Cote, or Toothpick Cote as he was called. Roger always had a toothpick in his mouth, even during games.

Practical jokes were a big thing and players could get away with stuff they could not even try in today's game. Roger was at the head of the class in pulling practical jokes, but somehow, he was never caught. You just assumed he was the culprit.

In the late 1960s and into the early 1970s, players did not wear helmets as a rule, and most guys either had full or partial dentures. Before practice, the players would take out their teeth and put them in the stall above the bench where they sat.

One day after practice, the guys came in and showered and started to put their teeth back in. The only problem was someone had moved all the dentures around, so guys were trying to fit some other player's teeth in their mouths.

It was hysterical. The only way we assumed it was Cote was because he'd left the ice early after blocking a Dave Amadio slap shot.

My first year, I was only 20, but I found out that was not going to stop me from becoming one of the guys, which meant never saying no when it was time to go for beers. That was every day when we didn't have a game.

Our normal routine was a morning practice followed by lunch and beer at the Elbow Lounge in Agawam. You would go home for an afternoon nap and then meet up later at another gin mill to start pounding the beer again. Some guys could obviously consume more than others, and there were too many times I tried to keep up with them.

One player on our 1969 team was Real "Frenchy" Lemieux, and to say he loved his beer was an understatement. One night after a home game we were boarding the bus for Rochester. Coach Wilson told the guys that because we had a game the next night, there was to be no drinking on the bus.

Most guys were already seated when Frenchy came on carrying a briefcase. He told the guys he had some business to catch up on, then took his normal seat on the back of the bus.

We had just pulled out of the Coliseum parking lot when Frenchy opened his briefcase. He had found a way to insert cup holders where he could easily place his 12-pack of Pabst Blue Ribbon. He drank the beer before we hit the Massachusetts Turnpike and never shared a drop.

You can't talk about hockey in Springfield without mentioning Rob Murray, one of the most intense players to ever lace on the skates in this city. Along with John Stevens, he provided the Falcons with their first captains in 1994.

What Rob lacked in offensive skill or skating speed, he made up with hard work, a desire to win at all costs and a tenacity to play hard every single shift, whether it was a game or practice.

I have many wonderful memories of Rob as a player for the Falcons, but I think what happened in the AHL All-Star game truly sums up what Rob was all about.

As we know, an All-Star game is pretty much a yawner with scores in the double digits. You see more hits with people bumping into each other in the beer lines then you do in the games. That was true, at least, until Rob was selected to participate in the classic event in recognition of his long career.

The game was held at Saint John in New Brunswick with a sold-out crowd. On Rob's first shift, an opposing player came around the net with his head down, Rob came in from the other side and delivered a crashing hit that leveled the guy.

It was "game on," as they say, and it helped produce one of the best and most physical games in AHL All-Star history, thanks to Rob setting the tone early.

When we honored Rob before one of the Falcons games, my partner, Wayne LaChance and I wanted to make it a special night. We surprised him by bringing his family in from Canada and we had to get him something as a gift, but we had no clue of what it was going to be.

We knew he had a cottage north of Toronto where he spent his summers, so we decided we would buy him a canoe - not just any canoe but the biggest frigging canoe we could find. We brought it out to center ice during the ceremony, not even giving a thought as to how he would get it home after the season was over.

I have never asked him, but if he didn't use it, I hope at least he took it back to Dick's Sporting Goods and picked himself up something or got the cash back.

My ideas of gifts are sometimes a little off the charts. Just ask Ralphie Calvanese, our long-time equipment manager.

Ralphie Calvanese is a fixture in the AHL, having served as an equipment manager in Springfield since the mid-1970s. He started as a stick boy and worked his

Rob Murray. (The Republican file photo).

way up to head equipment manager, a title he still held as of the 2018-19 season. Far and away the best in the business, he has turned down many opportunities to go to the NHL, but he is a local guy who was just happy working in his own backyard.

I worked closely with Ralph for over 30 years and when we purchased the Falcons, it was a no-brainer that he would stay on as long as he wanted. The "old goat" as he was affectionately called, had a lifetime contract with me and he never had to worry about job security.

We did have our moments. It was never over job performance, but sometimes I had to settle him down when his temper got the best of him. He could be a miserable son-of-a-gun at times. Sometimes it was all for show, just so he could make a point. Ralphie took pride in his dressing room and he made sure every player did as well. If you didn't, you would find out about it, and quickly.

One year, we had a first-round draft pick who was assigned to Springfield. Ralphie always made sure the players knew what to with their equipment when practice was over, and everything had to be hung just right.

The rookie made the mistake of just piling his sweaty underwear, equipment and skates in a pile in front of his locker and left the building. When he came in the next day, he had no equipment for practice and confronted Ralph.

The Old Goat screamed at him in front of the entire team, just to send a message: it didn't matter if you were a first-rounder or just a guy in on a tryout. Everyone was expected to treat their uniform and the dressing room with respect. Just for the record, the rookie found all of his equipment in the garbage can where the Old Goat had thrown it.

Even though the Goat had a lifetime contract, we still negotiated a deal every year. More than anything, it gave us a chance to have lunch after the season and just shoot the breeze about everything.

For whatever reason, we started going to "lunch" to talk about his contract at one of the strip clubs Ralphie was known to frequent during his single days. We would sit at the bar, have a beer, talk over his contract and never had a shortage of one-dollar bills. As the years went on, we had run out of clubs in the Springfield area and started heading south to Hartford.

The last contract we ever negotiated was at a gentlemen's club about 30 minutes north of Springfield, one I had never heard of, and it was about 12:30 in the afternoon. We were the only ones in the place, other than one young lady doing her thing on the stage.

I wanted to leave because we always did eat something, but this place didn't serve food and I am not sure I would have eaten it, anyway. The old Goat told me to sit tight as he had to make a call.

He came back and sat down, and we started talking. I had his past contracts on the bar beside my beer and went over some numbers. About 20 minutes later, a

Guest of Honor Springfield Falcons' Rob Murray during a pre game ceremony held in honor of his 1000th career game, on hand with him was his wife Caroline, holding their son Zachery, their daughter Taylor, (his sister Cory hidden in photo) his mother, Denise, right and Bruce Landon, second from right was the master of ceremony. Some of the gifts Murray received were a canoe and the television at right, Feb. 28, 2003.
(Photo by Mark M. Murray, The Republican).

Domino's Pizza guy came in and brought over a "greasy wheel."

Ralphie's phone call had been to order a pizza. There we sat with a pizza on a stool between us, and the new contract Ralphie had just signed.

In 1989-90 when we were chasing down our first of back-to-back Calder Cups, we had a saying used as motivation in the locker room and in the front office. It simply said, "Whatever It Takes." This just meant that it did not matter what it was going to take to win, we would find a way.

We had buttons made up for everyone to wear and it became our mantra for the playoffs. As we found out, Ralphie may have been taking this to the extreme, although it was never proven.

We were in the finals against Rochester, and we were trying to wrap up the series and the Calder Cup at home on a very hot and humid night. This was years before renovations were done at the Civic Center, so the building had a very old heating and air conditioning system.

After we had won the game and the Cup, we found out the Rochester players were almost having heat stroke in their dressing room between periods. What appeared to have happened is that someone had cranked up the heat in the room to an almost unbearable temperature. No one could substantiate it, but we wondered if the Old Goat had somehow been involved. Whatever it took.

We finally honored Ralphie for his years of service and arranged for nice tributes from players who had played in Springfield, as well as from the league office. Once again, I was under the gun to get him something for this special night, and I was clueless.

But Ralphie always referred himself to the Old Goat. When you called his office, that was the message you would even get on his phone. So, I figured what the hell, the guy needs his own goat. I purchased a goat in his honor and donated it to the Forest Park Zoo in Springfield. It lives in a stall bearing his name, Ralphie, the Old Goat.

Those who followed hockey in the 1960s and into the 1970s in Springfield will remember Coliseum Charlie, who practically became a household name to Springfield fans for his antics at every Indians game. Charlie used to sit in a section behind the net at the old barn, where he would get an early start to consuming as many beers as they could sell him. He would line the cups up on the ledge in front of his seat.

Usually sometime in the third period, the fun would begin. Charlie always wore a white shirt and after the beer kicked in, he would strip down to his tee shirt, and start waving his white shirt and let out his special rant. It fired up the crowd who anxiously waited for Charlie to do his thing.

One night, Charlie decided to bring a young lady to the game with him and she also got pretty seriously into the beer. Sure enough, off came Charlie's shirt and the young lady decided to follow suit and strip down to her bra.

That may have been the game that ended Charlie's cheerleading days in Springfield.

During the NHL lockout in the early 2000s, the Falcons played a game against Philadelphia's AHL team in Tampa Bay. I was in line at the concession stand and I heard someone yell out "Hey, Boo."

My nickname from my Kings playing days in Springfield had been Boo, but more than 30 years had passed, and I could think of no one in Tampa who would have known that. I turned around and there was Coliseum Charlie, all dressed up in a nice black suit. We reminisced for a few minutes about his days in Springfield.

Charlie passed away a few years later. Every city has their own "super fan" but there was no one quite like Coliseum Charlie - truly one of the great characters in Springfield hockey history.

Over the years, and especially when I was involved with the hockey side of the operation, I forged some great relationships with NHL teams and their personnel

Danny Briere (The Republican file photo).

that continue to this day. However, despite my best efforts, I was never able to connect with Wayne Gretzky, arguably the greatest hockey player of all time.

During the early years, we were associated with the Phoenix Coyotes, who at that time were owned by Richard Burke. His son, Taylor Burke, was their assistant general manager and responsible for Springfield players.

Taylor was very inexperienced, and he knew it, so he leaned on me to assist him as he learned the hockey side of the business. We struggled during those seasons and the Phoenix general manager, Mike Barnett, gave me more lip service and double-talk than any other GM with whom I'd been associated.

Barnett had represented Gretzky when he was a player agent, and Gretzky was working for the Coyotes. Since our team was playing so poorly and fans were staying away, I thought it would be a good idea if we could convince Gretzky to come to Springfield and get a chance to watch his prospects play. He would also be a good attraction for us, and his appearance would boost attendance for one game.

We agreed to donate $10,000 to a charity of his choice if he came to Springfield. We never got a response from him, one way or another.

There were also some bright spots in the early days, and one of them was getting a chance to watch a young Danny Briere. Danny is on my all-time top-5 list of players who put on skates in Springfield, not just because of his outstanding hockey abilities, but for his personality and the way he carried himself away from the rink.

There is one particular story that pretty much sums up Danny's nature as a special person. One day, a youth hockey team from Pittsfield attended a practice in Springfield, but one young player was sick and unable to attend.

Briere was his favorite player. When Danny heard about this, and without anyone knowing about it, he drove on his own to Pittsfield to watch the young boy practice.

After it was over, he went down to the dressing room to introduce himself. He totally surprised and thrilled the young Danny Briere fan.

Several years later, after Danny had retired, we were holding a "Blast from the Past Night." I thought it would be great if he would come in, sign autographs and drop the ceremonial first puck. This is the type of thing some hockey players don't like to do. I called Danny and asked him if we could pay him to come in for the game. We would also provide a car service to pick him up. He told me he would check his schedule and get back to me.

The next day, Danny called me back and said he would attend, and did not want anything in return. He also said he would drive himself and did not need a car service. He said he was honored we would think of him, and that he was so grateful for his time in Springfield that he felt it was the least he could do to pay us back.

One of the other good guys we had the pleasure of watching was John Stevens. John was not the most talented defenseman in the game, but he was as tough as they come. He was a tremendous leader who served as our captain, as did forward Rob Murray.

John was a great teacher for the young guys, and it was not a surprise that he went on to become a coach in the NHL.

Dr. David Page, a retired surgeon and good friend of mine, was our covering doctor at one game and shared a story over lunch with me about John, one that I won't forget.

John had received a horrible cut to the chin and lip during the game and went to the dressing room to be attended. Dr. Page took one look at the cut and told John there was no way he could stitch that bad of a cut on a table in the dressing room, which meant John would have to go to the hospital.

According to Dr. Page, John picked his bleeding head off the table, looked him right in the eye and said, "Doc, you fix this (expletive deleted) cut right here or I am going to stick a Band-Aid on it and go back to the bench." That was the competitor in John Stevens.

Dr. Page also recalled watching the Los Angeles Kings play on television and Stevens was coaching. They had a closeup of John, and the scar was hardly visible. Dr. Page was pretty proud of his work.

Not every player who came through Springfield has a funny story attached to his name. There are just some guys who are worth mentioning because of the first-class way they represented themselves and our franchise. Ryan Craig is one of those guys and another member of my all-time top -5 list of players who played in Springfield.

Ryan had two stints in Springfield, over 300 games in all. In 2004, he was assigned to us when we were affiliated with the Tampa Bay Lightning. Then in 2012, when the Columbus Blue Jackets (our new NHL affiliate) were looking for a veteran guy, they went after Craig.

In my eyes, Ryan ranks as one of the best captains I have ever been around. He personified leadership on and off the ice. What he lacked in speed as a player, he made up in hockey smarts, a willingness to play the game in the dirty areas and a passion for winning at all costs.

Everybody in the locker room looked up to him. He taught the younger players how to dress, how to act, how to respect their teammates and training staff, and to hold themselves accountable at all times.

The importance of that cannot be understated and shows itself in many ways. At the end of the season, players are responsible for tipping the trainer and equipment manager. The amounts vary, usually based on what the player is earning.

However, that is not always the case. One year, we had a player making an NHL-level salary who skipped out at the end of the year. Not only was there no tip, there was not even a goodbye.

Ryan would make sure that would never happen during his watch as captain. At the end of the season, he would call a team meeting and although most players knew what their responsibility would be, he would guide the young players as to how much they were expected to shell out - always keeping in mind the individual player's salary so it would not be too much of a burden.

I became close to Ryan over the years, especially when he knew his career was coming to an end. He was one of the guys who loved to sit in my office and talk hockey, trades and coaching, and he soaked up everything. He always wanted to know what was going on in the league and it was certainly no surprise when he told me he wanted to stay in hockey after his playing days were over.

He started preparing for it by keeping a daily journal of everything and everyone associated with the game. It was no shock to me when the new NHL expansion team, the Golden Knights, in Las Vegas tabbed him to be one of their assistant coaches. His years as a team captain, leader and great person paid off and I couldn't be happier for him. Good things happen to good people.

Bruce "Gabby" Boudreau went on to become one of the most successful coaches in the National Hockey League. He paid his dues with coaching stints and success in the ECHL, the old International Hockey League and the AHL before he made it to the "show."

As of 2019, he was behind the bench with the Minnesota Wild. The only unfulfilled goal of his great coaching career was that he had yet to win a Stanley Cup.

As previously mentioned, Bruce came to Springfield as a player in 1987. The way we got him signed is pretty interesting. Indians owner Peter Cooney had decided he wanted to sign two of our own players and not just depend on our NHL affiliate. Although we did not have a big budget, we decided we would go after a top-line forward and if possible a steady, dependable defenseman.

We set our sights on Boudreau and were going to go all out to sign him, even if it meant we had no money left for another player. I tracked Gabby down and made the first call.

He was on the golf course. I introduced myself, even though it was not necessary because Boudreau probably knows every player who ever played the game. I had to start somewhere, so I made him a low-ball offer. He was polite but declined the offer and told me he was in talks with another team. I told him to at least think about joining us and I would call him back.

I waited only about thirty minutes and called him on the golf course again. This time, I upped the offer considerably, but I knew it was still below what we would have to pay him. It did attract his interest as he now knew I was serious, but again he turned it down. He mentioned he was going to sign another deal but had not closed it yet.

I had set the hook with my latest offer, but now I had to reel him in. I did not give him much time because I wanted to finalize the deal while he was still on the course. I figured by now, his golfing buddies would be ticked off that he was taking so many calls when they were in their back swing. I did not want him to have time to call the other team and start playing one deal against the other.

I called again, bumped the offer to really make him think about it and told him it was my final offer. He told me that if I made it a two-year deal, he would accept. I added another year without even talking to Peter about it, and we had locked up one of the most prolific goal scorers in the history of the league.

We still had a little cash left in the can to sign defenseman John Mokosak. Gabby Boudreau is one of my best friends in hockey to this day. He still doesn't know (until now, perhaps) that if he had held out for at least one more hole, we would have blown our entire budget to get him signed.

I think it was in the early to mid-1980s that AHL teams started having more Europeans on their rosters. They came here looking to making the big money in the NHL, but often found themselves being assigned to the minors. A European player did not spend many consecutive years in the AHL. If he did not make it to the NHL in very short time, he normally returned to his home country.

To the Europeans, playing in the NHL is the ultimate reward and well worth the sacrifices required. However, for most of them, playing in the AHL was no better

Falcon Ryan Craig, Springfield Falcons All-Time Goal Scorer with Bruce Landon at an awards ceremony at center ice prior to the Falcons vs. Portland game at the MassMutual Center, April 2, 2015. (Photo by David Molnar, The Republican).

than staying with their European club, especially if they knew their chance of making it to the major league was not in the cards.

Over the years, every AHL general manager with whom I spoke had a story or two about the "Euros" on his team. We were no exception. I hate to generalize, but many of them were very high maintenance.

In some cases, it was a language issue, especially with the guys from Russia or the Czechs. You could understand that. Unfortunately, some of them did not make the adjustment and needed a lot of babysitting.

We had a young defenseman, Anton Blomqvist, a Columbus draft pick from Sweden who came to us in 2010. Here was a rookie playing in North America for the first time, and he was a really great kid. You could almost feel sorry for him as he struggled at times on the ice, and in making the adjustment away from the rink.

With every player, we tried our best to help them get settled. It meant helping them find a place to live and hoping like hell they would go in with another player, which was not always the case. For some reason, I always found the Swedes liked to live by themselves. They always wanted to rent or buy a car. It didn't matter to them that in most cases, you had to be 25 to be able to rent a vehicle.

It especially didn't bother Anton. He was hell-bent on having a car when he was here. I was able to set him up with a friend of mine who looked the other way and would rent clunkers to some of the players. It was basic transportation, which is all they really needed.

One day, Anton came in my office with a sheepish look on his face. He brought with him over $300 in tickets he had received in the mail. and he had no idea what they were for. I told him I would look into it and get back to him.

I found out he'd been going to Boston on a regular basis to visit a friend of his who played for the Bruins. He would drive up to the toll booth and see the "Fast Lane" sign. He did not have a transponder and he just thought he was supposed to drive faster through the toll booth. The mystery of the tickets was solved.

It was not unusual for a European player to rent a car and then just leave at the end of the year without ever returning the car. More than once, I would receive a call from my car-rental friend to track down one of his cars.

One year, we had a player who wanted to buy a brand-new Jeep and did not care what it cost. He had a pretty good signing bonus and was eager to spend it. I tried to talk him out of it and explained it would cost him a lot of money to ship it back to his hometown. He didn't care, so I sent him off by himself to visit a dealership.

I wanted to go with him to help negotiate the deal, but he said he would take care of it. He drove in the next day in a top-of-the-line SUV, for which he paid full price. At the end of the season, he did not even bother trying to ship it home. He just flew home and left it in the driveway of the house he was renting.

He did call back a few weeks later and told me he was sending the keys to a friend of his that he met in Springfield. I have no clue what happened after that, nor did I really care.

Unfortunately, some - not all - of the Russian players assigned to Springfield had trouble staying away from the vodka. In 1992, we added a big Russian kid, Leonid Toropchenko who was 6-foot-4 and 225 pounds. He was a powerful skater with a booming shot, and in his first year, he scored 31 goals for us.

He showed enough ability for us to think he was going to be a future NHL star. Jay Leach was our coach and we had a good enough regular season to make it to the playoffs. On the morning of our first home playoff game, the guys were out for their pregame practice and I was in my office when Leach came barreling through the door with his skates still on.

"Where in the hell is Torpo?" he was screaming. I had no idea, but Jay told me he did not show up for practice and I had to find him. After making a couple of calls, I found out the big Russian was dating a lady who worked at Theodore's Restaurant in downtown Springfield. I was able to track down her number, and luckily was able to get in touch with her. I asked her if she knew where we could find Torpo.

"He is passed out in my bedroom upstairs," she said. I got the address from her and went out to the ice to tell Jay. He took his skates off, threw on some shoes and away we went up to her apartment.

When we got there, Jay told me to wait downstairs; he would take care of the situation. A few minutes later, Leach came flying down the stairs and told me we were leaving.

When we got to my car, he started laughing so hard, snot bubbles were coming out his nose. As the story was told to me, he had gone into the bedroom and the big guy was out cold. He started shaking him to wake him up. Finally, this hulk of a man rolled over, looked up and said, "Coach, Torpo bad boy," and then rolled over and went back to sleep.

On the way back to the arena, coach was not sure whether to suspend him or send him home. He didn't really know what to do, but since Torpo was our best offensive player, he decided to let the players decide.

After a team meeting, the guys decided to let him play, but he would pay a hefty fine for missing practice. He made it on time to the game and never showed any signs of a hangover.

After he left us, Toropchenko played one season in Cleveland of the IHL before finishing his career in Russia. His promising NHL chances never happened, and his pro career here was all too short.

Not all the characters of the game or in the game are coaches, players, trainers or even management people. There are the Coliseum Charlies and the special fans who always made things interesting.

There were also the people who volunteered their time, year after year - like our outstanding off-ice officials. These guys were responsible for being timekeepers, official scorers, statisticians and handling other game-night responsibilities.

One of the highlights and truly fun times during my hectic career was stopping by almost every game in the press room and shooting the breeze with these guys. The stories were endless, and the back-and-forth barbs never stopped.

The late Richard Sacenti was a long-time goal judge going back to the days when I played. He was a goal judge in my first pro game in 1969 and spent over 50 years putting on the red light. As the years went by, so did his eyesight. So affectionately he became known as Trigger.

That was because he would often turn on the light before the puck had even crossed the goal line. Sometimes it never did, but the light would still go on.

Richard became the target of many of our one-liners. We told him he was suffering from premature illumination. We told him he would listen to the sound of the crowd before he would turn the light on and if he ever lost his hearing, he would really be sunk.

But Trigger could give it back as well as he could take it, and he reminded me on many nights of how really lousy I'd been in goal. He always had a big bear hug for me and an infectious laugh that I only wish I could replicate.

Poor health finally forced Richard to give up his stool behind the net. He always wore a tie with hockey players on it at every game. After he had retired from being a goal judge, he showed up at my office and gave me his hockey tie, which to this day is one of the most touching things that has ever happened to me in my career.

When I retired, I donated over 50 ties to a charity, but Trigger's hockey tie will always hang proudly in my closet.

22
AFFILIATIONS

Fans were always wondering why it seemed Springfield could never get one NHL team to partner up with and stay for a long time, similar to what Providence had with Boston. We changed affiliations often, sometimes when it was our decision, but often it was based on money or the NHL club thinking they could strike a better deal somewhere else.

It's important to understand that over the years, the philosophy of the NHL clubs changed often as to where they wanted their AHL team located. For many years, they didn't care how far apart the NHL and AHL cities were, as long as the NHL team received an acceptable affiliation fee and their players had a chance to develop in the right environment. Things started to change when NHL management in many cities decided it wanted its AHL farm team closer to the big club.

These executives believed it was easier for player call-ups and assignments, and easier for the scouting department to keep an eye on the development of their players. You can make the argument that despite the distance, affiliations worked well for years with the Los Angeles Kings in Manchester, New Hampshire and the Toronto Maple Leafs in St. John's, Newfoundland.

However, as we well know, nothing much stays the same from year to year in the American Hockey League and adapting to the demands of the NHL is nothing new.

Along the way, I made some mistakes in my decisions to change affiliations. Usually, it was out of frustration for our lack of success on the ice, and patience has never been my strong suit.

The best case in point was when we agreed to part company with Tampa Bay and hook our wagon to the Edmonton Oilers. That's one I'd like back.

Springfield Falcons president and general manager Bruce Landon, speaks at the podium during a press conference announcing the affiliation with the Edmonton Oilers hockey team, Mar. 19, 2007. (Photo by Mark M. Murray, The Republican).

Press conference at the Naismith Memorial Basketball Hall of Fame to announce new affiliation between the Springfield Falcons of the American Hockey League with the Tampa Bay Lightning of the National Hockey League. Jay Feaster, vice president and general manager of the Lightning speaking during press conference with Bruce Landon, at right, Falcons president and general manager, Feb. 5, 2004.
(Photo by Michael S. Gordon, The Republican).

The Tampa Bay Lightning were being run by Jay Feaster, a long-time AHL executive with the Hershey Bears and someone I really respected. Jay and I agreed on a five-year contract with him promising to deliver a competitive and exciting team to Springfield.

It was a speech I heard way too many times from NHL general managers. To Jay's credit, he opened his wallet and signed five really good veterans for us. The problem was that at this time, Tampa Bay had a horrible drafting record and had very few prospects.

It has been proven over and over that to be successful at the AHL level, you need the right mix of veterans and first- and second-year pros. Despite Jay's efforts and numerous trips to Springfield for meetings with me, we could not find the right formula to work.

My patience and that of our fans was running out. Jay was also getting frustrated and it truly bothered him that he was letting me down, so we made the decision that if we couldn't find a way to make it work, we would part company.

Jay Feaster, vice president and general manager of the Lightning, Feb. 5, 2004. (Photo by Michael S. Gordon, The Republican).

In hindsight, I made a move that never should have happened.

A call was made to league president Dave Andrews, who normally gets involved in orchestrating affiliation changes. Dave told me that Edmonton was looking to make a change that looked a good fit because Scott Howson, who, I had known from his playing days in Springfield, was their new assistant general manager.

Scott and I met over a couple of beers at the AHL All-Star game in Toronto and talked about a long-term agreement between Edmonton and Springfield. At the same time, Andrews was helping Feaster work on a deal to have Norfolk, Virginia become the new farm team for the Lightning.

As they say, the grass is not always greener on the other side of the fence. While

Chris MacFarland, assistant general manager of the National Hockey League's Columbus Blue Jackets, talks about their new affiliation with the Springfield Falcons at the MassMutual Center on March 25, 2010. (Photo by Michael S. Gordon, The Republican).

Edmonton turned out to be pretty much of a disaster for us, Tampa enjoyed success with Norfolk eventually winning a Calder Cup.

Sometimes, we could not keep an NHL partner because they made up their mind, for whatever reason, that they could find a better deal somewhere else, or that another city would be better for their players. Even though we still had time on our contract with Edmonton, I received a call from their president, Patrick LaForge, who had sprayed all sorts of negative commentary to the Edmonton press about the city of Springfield.

Patrick went off on how bad it was for his players, and that did not sit well with me. I ripped into him for going public with such stupidity. But he was laying the

The Springfield Falcons held an "Interactive Hockey Event" at Tower Square where fans could meet players and participate in "floor hockey" challenges. Here, 7 year-old Jonathan Cimino of Wilbraham gets some stick instruction from Falcons' defenseman Bryan Helmer, Feb. 20, 2013. (Photo by Don Treeger, The Republican).

groundwork, because he wanted to relocate to Oklahoma City where he had visions of large crowds and where they expected to make a lot of money. He found out quickly that Springfield was not such a bad place after all.

Oklahoma City had such a tough travel schedule that it took its toll on his players, something that was never a problem in Springfield. The Oilers also lost a bucket load of money. As it turned out, Oklahoma City did not last long in the league.

With Edmonton deciding to leave, I once again had to find a partner for us. Our selling points have always been our easy travel schedule, our history of paying our affiliation fees on time - which many other cities at the time did not do - and a nice facility with most of our practice time in our own arena. I also like to think that players knew when they came to Springfield, they would be treated right.

Scott Howson had left the Oilers to become the new general manager of the Columbus Blue Jackets, and it did not take a long negotiation for us to hammer out a deal.

For me, personally, this was a great move. Scott was very honest, direct and sincere in providing the budget that would allow them to sign good players for us and - just as importantly - provide us with solid coaching. That was something Edmonton had failed to do.

It also gave me the opportunity to work closely with Chris MacFarland, their assistant general manager. In most cases with independent ownership in the AHL, the NHL team runs the hockey side of the business and local management takes care of the business side.

Chris respected my years of hockey experience and allowed me to really get involved in hockey decisions, which was the fun part of the game. We reviewed free agents together in the offseason and I was directly involved in dealing with our ECHL affiliate.

One of the more interesting signings in the offseason came when Chris said he wanted to sign Bryan Helmer, who was getting up in age but still a perennial All-Star defenseman. Chris thought he would not only help us on the ice but set a good example for the young kids.

We thought we had him signed, but Helmer was holding out for one thing he wanted in his contract. It was not cash or a bonus for points scored. He wanted a new Xbox to give to his kids.

I was handling all the AHL contracts and Chris called me up and said, "Give him a freakin' Xbox, but don't dare put it in the contract." We got Helmer signed. I went out and bought him the Xbox.

However, good things come to an end and the time came when I was forced to make another big decision about our affiliation. Columbus management loved it in Springfield for all the right reasons, but they had an opportunity to move their development club to Cleveland. That would allow them to brand their NHL and

AHL teams under the same banner of the same state, Ohio, and in close proximity.

At the time, a big swing was going on with affiliations and my decision was going to impact not just Springfield, but my AHL partners in San Antonio, Cleveland and NHL teams Columbus, Colorado and Arizona. I was holding the trump card and getting pressure to let Columbus out of its last year of the agreement with Springfield.

I really wanted to make Columbus finish out its last year in Springfield, but in doing so, we would have been a lame-duck franchise. I have always felt you need to have the stomach to stand up for what you believe is right. Hindsight, as they say, is 20/20 and as it turns out I made one of the worst decisions of my AHL management career.

I let Columbus leave for Cleveland, but not before I was able to sign a long-term deal with Arizona. It turned out to be a disaster. Columbus' farm team went on to win a Calder Cup in Cleveland, and Arizona stuck it to me by giving us a very bad team. It was the beginning of the end for the Springfield Falcons.

It is somewhat ironic that the Falcons started in 1994 with Winnipeg, and later with Phoenix, where the Winnipeg Jets moved in 1996. We also had players from the Hartford Whalers, in that first year of 1994.

The Falcons ended their time in Springfield with Arizona (which had replaced "Phoenix" with the state name in 2014) as their NHL partner. There were quite a few positives to it, too.

We did have some success with Phoenix in the early years, and I had the opportunity to watch a young player like Daniel Briere win rookie-of-the-year honors. Daniel went on to a great NHL career, and to this day, he's in my personal top-5 of all-time favorites to have played in Springfield.

The Coyotes also provided us with Rob Murray, one of the best captains ever to put on a Springfield uniform. Rob is also in my all-time top-5 of favorites.

I built one of my best longstanding hockey relations when I was able to work with Laurence Gilman, who had taken over as the Phoenix assistant GM. He was the guy with whom I worked closely with during a few of those Phoenix years.

There were really tough seasons on the ice, though, and Laurence had to take the brunt of it. We used to have town hall meetings with fans before some of the home games, and when Laurence came to town, he'd face the angry mob or "stalkers" as he used to affectionately call them.

Laurence and I share a bond with some memories of a few of the bad signings by Phoenix. One summer, we were at our annual meeting at Hilton Head, S.C., and Laurence and I were playing golf. The league meetings normally fall right around the same time as the NHL free agency period, which starts on July 1.

Most of the NHL general managers and assistant GMs are glued to their phones during this time, and Gilman was no exception. We were in the middle of the fairway on the 16th hole, and Laurence was getting ready to hit his second shot when his phone rang.

After a couple of minutes, he threw his phone down, started jumping up and down and screamed that Phoenix had just signed Peter Fabus. I joined in the celebration, even though I had absolutely no clue who Peter Fabus was.

After we stopped making complete idiots of ourselves, Laurence explained that Fabus was a hotshot center out of the Czech Republic. Fabus ended up playing a total of 39 games with us, with the grand total of five goals.

A few years after we had ended our affiliation agreement with Phoenix, I sent Laurence a player jersey. It was the one worn by Peter Fabus, except I had changed the name on the sweater to say "Fabust." It summed up his career in Springfield.

I can stick in the needle and be a real you-know-what at times.

Laurence and I remain great friends and as of 2019, he was serving as assistant GM of the Toronto Maple Leafs.

We were forced to change affiliations several times during the years of the Falcons, as the Indians had done before us, but we still had the chance to watch players hone their skills as they prepared for an NHL career. There are so many such players that it is impossible to talk about them all.

We have always been blessed in Springfield with great goaltending. We had one goaltender who started his pro career in Springfield in 1994 with the Falcons and ended his career in 2012 with the Falcons.

Manny Legace was a Hartford Whalers draft pick who went on to play 367 games in the NHL, winning a Stanley Cup and also being named an NHL All-Star. Manny is also in my personal top-5 of all-time guys to play in Springfield. He comes to town every summer to be my golf partner in a big four-ball tournament.

It was not just the Falcons who seemed to change affiliations every year. The Indians had done so as well. Unless you check the record book, it's hard to keep track of them all but Washington, Chicago, the New York Rangers, New York Islanders, Los Angeles, Boston, Hartford, Philadelphia, Minnesota and even the old Kansas City Scouts put players in Springfield at one time or another.

The Scouts are mostly forgotten today, and many young fans don't even know they existed. But they played as an NHL team from 1974 to 1976 before moving to Colorado (not as the Avalanche, but as the Rockies), before finally becoming the New Jersey Devils.

It would make a good trivia question to ask sometime over a few beers: how many NHL teams have put players in Springfield?

I was fortunate to have had the opportunity to work with some of the best hockey people in the NHL, and over the years I had a chance to get to know most of the scouts who came to Springfield. During our Chicago affiliation in the early 1980s, I received a call from Bob Pulford, the long-time general manager of the Blackhawks.

Bob is not exactly Mr. Warmth and is a man of very few words. He told me to keep an eye out for his head pro scout, Jim Pappin, who was coming in to watch their prospects.

During the second period, I was watching the game in the press box with our owner, Peter Cooney, and I asked him if he had seen Pappin. He said he had not. That was true until we looked toward a nearby section and saw this guy stretched over two rows of seats - sound asleep, while the game was going on.

It was Pappin, out like a light. Cooney and I laughed until it hurt and could not help wondering what his scouting report to Pulford was going to look like.

Many pro scouts are former NHL or AHL players who have latched on to a nice job after their playing careers have ended. One of the standard lines around the scouting circles is "What are the six words that a pro scout has never heard?" The answer is: "Last minute to go in the game."

Scouts are notorious for packing up their computers and notes and heading out before the game comes to an end. The late Garnet "Ace" Bailey, who was tragically killed in the 9/11 terrorist attacks, drove from his home in the Boston area to scout frequently at the Springfield games.

Most teams provide a press room for scouts, media and off-ice officials to gather before the game. Usually, some food is provided. One night, Ace was coming in to scout Springfield but first made a stop in Worcester. At the time, they used to serve up practically a five-course meal in their press room before games. Ace put on the feed bag in Worcester before driving the rest of the way to Springfield.

I can't say I blame him because back in the Indians days, we served up soggy hot dogs and coffee that tasted like pond water on a humid day.

Because of Springfield's location, it is easy for NHL brass to come to town to watch their minor league players. In 1981-82, we were affiliated with the New York Rangers and their coach, Herb Brooks, came to town. He did not pick the best of times.

Brooks had become a legend by coaching the 1980 U.S. Olympic gold medal team, but that didn't matter to the fans in Springfield at the time. The Rangers had given us one of the worst teams we have ever seen in Springfield.

It was at the end of the first period, and I had come upstairs from the office when I saw what I thought was a big brawl taking place on the concourse. We were down 4-0 and the fans were taking out their frustrations on Herb, pinning him against the wall with an angry mob circling around him so he could not escape.

It looked like a scene out of a Gunsmoke TV episode, where Sheriff Matt Dillon was called on to break up a gang that was ready to lynch someone. Thankfully, nothing physical took place, but the fans verbally let the gold-medal coach know how they felt about his Ranger players.

It was the first and last time Herb made the visit to Springfield for a game.

Finding stability and holding on to one affiliation was never easy. In most cases,

Herb Brooks.

An event to announce the name of the new Springfield AHL hockey team "The Thunderbirds" was held on June 15, 2016 at the MassMutual Center. This is Dave Andrews, President of the American Hockey League. (Photo by Don Treeger, The Republican).

money played a major role. That was why Cooney decided to switch from the Islanders to the Whalers.

Having provided us with a Calder Cup champion in 1990, the Islanders wanted a major hike in their affiliation fee. We switched to the Whalers and won again in 1991.

When we switched from Columbus to Edmonton, money was again one of the reasons. We knew we had the Oilers by the throats, because at the time, they had nowhere else to go. We leveraged that into getting a really good financial deal.

Over the years, the cost of doing business for independently owned AHL teams has risen dramatically, and if not for the great work by AHL president

Garnet "Ace" Bailey, 53, director of pro scouting for the Los Angeles Kings ice hockey team, shown in a handout photo taken in Sept. 2000, was among those killed Tuesday, Sept. 11, 2001, when two hijacked airliners slammed into the World Trade Center in New York. Bailey and Mark Bavis, an amateur scout for the team, were aboard United Airlines Flight 175, the second plane to hit the World Trade Center according to Mike Altieri, the team's public relations director. (AP Photo/Los Angeles Kings, Juan Ocampo).

Dave Andrews the costs would have reached the point of driving some AHL teams out of business. Each team negotiates its own deals, but as costs started to rise, Dave stepped in and held a number of meetings with the NHL brass to present a case as to how their demands were impacting the AHL and causing hardship for independent owners.

Affiliation fees are still high, but they have stabilized over the last few years.

One of my strengths was being able to negotiate deals that were always near the bottom in terms of payments to the NHL club. But sometimes, you get what you pay for, and a case can be made that some of our lousy teams were a result of my being too frugal.

Manny Legace, celebrated goaltender of the Springfield Falcons. (The Republican file photo).

Most AHL fans don't realize how the affiliation agreements work, and they do vary a little from city to city. AHL teams pay their NHL partner a flat fee with small adjustments or increases each year if it's a multi-year deal. As an example, our deal with Columbus started out at $750,000 and eventually reached $825,000.

For this, the NHL team provides the players, coach, assistant coach and head trainer. I always wanted to protect Ralph Calvanese, our long-time equipment manager, so we paid him directly.

The NHL club provides sticks, skates and most of the outer equipment. Springfield paid for jerseys, underwear ,socks and the like.

The NHL club also pays for all costs for call-ups and assignments. Springfield was responsible for all team travel, part of training camp costs and for the day-to-day operation of the franchise. There were always bonuses for performance and other smaller details in all the contracts, sometimes right down to who would pay for the Calder Cup rings.

Unfortunately, since 1991 - approaching 30 years at this writing - that has not been something Springfield has had to worry about. I hope that changes soon.

The landscape of the AHL has finally stabilized and I don't think you will ever see the volatility we witnessed previously. Through the work of Andrews, the league worked hard to a get to a model where the AHL would have the same number of teams as the NHL.

For the most part, this is a good thing as it stops the constant changing of affiliations. However, it can limit flexibility and if you are locked in with a partner who continues to give you poor teams year after year, or is very difficult to work with, headaches for the independent owners are inevitable. We saw that way too many times in Springfield.

Bruce Landon bobblehead at the MassMutual Center in Springfield on March 3, 2017. (Photo by Chris Marion, The Republican).

23
THE BIRTH OF THE THUNDERBIRDS

As I look back now on the Pompea years and the way it came to an end, it may have proven to be the best thing that could have happened. It opened the door for new excitement and a new and positive investment group that wanted to make sure that never again would we have to worry about Springfield losing its professional hockey team.

It all happened primarily because of Paul Picknelly, one of Springfield's leading businessmen and part of the family that own Peter Pan Bus Lines - the company whose bus had brought me to Springfield for the first time, when I began my pro career way back in 1969.

Forty-seven years later, in 2016, when news reached Paul's desk about the Arizona Coyotes moving our AHL franchise to Tuscon, he called me and asked me to meet with him. He asked me one question, "What are our chances of keeping hockey in Springfield?" He had already had a conversation with the league president, Dave Andrews, but now he wanted my help and I was more than willing to give it.

Paul was putting his investment team together. All I was doing was using my years of experience in negotiating leases and affiliation agreements, preparing operating budgets and sharing this information with Paul and two of his key people.

I also was giving him my own advice on how he would have to approach the purchase of the Portland, Maine franchise, which had gone up for sale. Buying it and moving it to Springfield was the only chance we had of keeping hockey in Springfield.

The rest, as they say, is history. Paul formed an impressive group, and, with the guidance of Dave Andrews, they were successful in their purchase and the relocation of the franchise.

Above: The Falcon mascot, Oct. 18, 2000. (Photo by David Molnar, The Republican.)

Right: "Screech" the Springfield Falcon's mascot with a little hockey fan at the game between the Albany Devils and the Springfield Falcons on Friday, April 3, 2015 at the MassMutual Center. (Photo by David Molnar, The Republican).

Springfield Falcons mascot "Screech" entertains the crowd during the team's season finale Sunday against the Portland Pirates at the MassMutual Center, April 18, 2016. (Photo by Chris Marion, courtesy Springfield Falcons)

Paul Picknelly and Lyman Wood at the ribbon-cutting ceremony to mark the official opening of The Amazing World of Dr. Seuss Museum at the Springfield Museums on June 2, 2017. (Photo by Don Treeger, The Republican).

The process was done in a remarkably short time and under the pressure of a tight deadline. I was content in knowing that one more time, and the last time it would be necessary, a successful effort had been made to make sure we would keep our beloved professional hockey team.

Andrews always supported our efforts to maintain an AHL franchise.
The league offices are in Springfield, a prize for a city that is much smaller than many which now belong to the league - Chicago, Milwaukee, San Antonio, San Diego, Cleveland and Toronto among them.

Bruce Landon (L) receives a commemorative jersey from Thunderbirds Senior Vice President Chris Thompson (R) during a pre-game tribute to Landon at the MassMutual Center in Springfield on March 3, 2017. (Photo by Chris Marion, The Republican/MassLive.com).

An event to announce the name of the new Springfield AHL hockey team "The Thunderbirds" was held on June 15, 2016 at the MassMutual Center. Bruce Landon, former owner of the Springfield Falcons hockey team acknowledges the crowd after it was announced that the street Falcons Way would be renamed Bruce Landon Way.
(Photo by Don Treeger, The Republican).

Falcons Bruce Landon announces his retirement from the team during a press conference at the MassMutual Center on Feb. 4, 2014. (Photo by Dave Roback, The Republican).

Springfield had also been in the AHL since 1936. Much of the league's history had been formed here. With the brief interruption of two years in the early 1950s, the city had never been without a team. Paul's investment and ownership team made sure it would stay where it belonged.

I was ready to retire, but Paul asked me to stay on for one year as a consultant to help the newly named Thunderbirds get off the ground. I could not say no, but I realized that for me, the end was near. I was ready for the next chapter in my life.

24
CLOSING

As I look back at my long career in hockey and for that matter my life, I find it interesting how one phone call can make such a profound difference.

If Larry Regan of the Los Angeles Kings had not called me at 2 a.m. one September night, I may have never made it to Springfield and never experienced the many opportunities that came my way. If Peter Cooney had not called me at home one night, while I was soaking in my hot tub, to tell me he sold the team, would I have ever had the chance to become an owner of an AHL team?

If my best buddy, Wayne LaChance, had not picked up the phone and called me after he heard the news of the sale of the Indians, would we have ever met to put an ownership group together? If a lawyer from New York City, Stuart Levy, had not called me from England to tell me he had an investor, would we have ever found that final piece of our investment team?

If Jack Kelly had not called me one day in June to tell me the Whalers had selected me in the WHA player draft and wanted to sign me, would I have ever enjoyed five of my most memorable years as a player? If Attorney George Leary had not called me when my World Hockey Association days were over and offered me a contract to play for Springfield and do some summer sales for him, would I have ever been given another chance to become a sports executive?

If Marcia Oliver had not taken my phone call, after I had mustered up the courage to pick up the phone to ask her out, would there have been a Mrs. Landon?

I have been very fortunate in my career to receive far more accolades than I deserved. The AHL Hall of Fame, the Massachusetts Hall of Fame, the Springfield Hockey Hall of Fame and the more recent Kingston, Ontario Hall of Fame are all honors I cherish.

Above: Nathan Costa, Executive Vice President of the Springfield Thunderbirds speaks while Bruce Landon looks on during ceremonies re-naming the street by the MassMutual Center as Bruce Landon Way, July 19, 2016. (Photo by Dave Roback, The Republican).

Right: Bruce Landon Way, July 19, 2016. (Photo by Dave Roback, The Republican).

Springfield Mayor Domenic J. Sarno speaks during ceremonies re-naming the street by the MassMutual Center as Bruce Landon Way, July 19, 2016. State Rep. Angelo Puppolo (L) and Nathan Costa look on. (Photo by Dave Roback, The Republican).

Above: Bruce Landon, center, watches as the street by the MassMutual Center was re-named Bruce Landon Way on July 19, 2016. At left is his wife Marcia and at right, his daughter Tracey Chrisanthopoulos. (Photo by Dave Roback, The Republican).

I always question, did I deserve them? I surrounded myself with really great people, who at times made me look better than I might have been.

It's said that unless you are the lead dog, the view never changes. I did relish the opportunity to be the guy in charge. When George Leary gave me my first chance to go in to the front office in 1977 with no experience, I made a promise to him. I said, "There are times when I will be outsmarted, but I will never be outworked."

If there is one thing I can be proud of, it's that I can look back and know I have lived up to that promise every minute of every day.

When you are in a position of relevance for so many years, it is not easy to fade into the shadows. No matter how humble you try to be, there is a part of you that still relishes being in the spotlight. Hockey for me was consuming for a very long time. It was an addiction. The only way I knew I could have peace of mind in my retirement years was to go cold turkey and stay away.

I don't miss the game. I am now over that. I will always miss being involved in the super people who were such a big part of my life in so many different ways.

I look back at the successes and the failures, the stupid decisions I made and the ones where I broke into my happy dance. Far too many times, I have said I don't want to live my life by looking through the rear-view mirror.

For me, writing this book and giving readers an inside look at a lifetime in hockey is the closure I need. I won't look back any longer, but I will look up at the sign in downtown Springfield that says "45 Bruce Landon Way" and be very proud of the work I put in to get there.

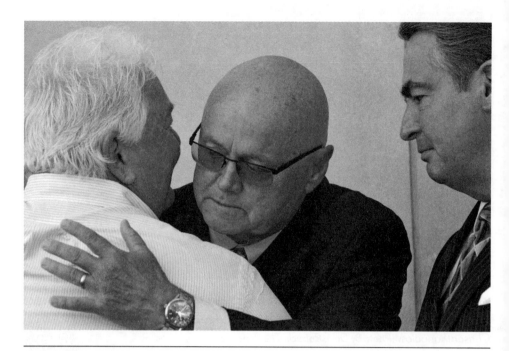

Paul Picknelly hugs Bruce Landon as Springfield Mayor Domenic J. Sarno looks on during ceremonies Tuesday re-naming the street by the MassMutual Center as Bruce Landon Way, July 19, 2016. (Photo by Dave Roback, The Republican).

Ben Zaranek, of Pope Francis High School, was awarded the Bruce Landon Award, during the Bessone Hockey Awards Banquet at the Dante Club in West Springfield, May 5, 2019. (Photo by Frederick Gore, The Republican).

David Tuohey, of the Exposition Area Scholarship Fund and a member of the Bessone Committee, addresses the crowd at the Bessone Hockey Awards Banquet at the Dante Club in West Springfield, May 5, 2019. Joining in the ceremony is Jason Kates, of MassLive, Bob Shore, presenter of the Eddie Shore Award, William Sapelli, chairman, Bruce Landon, presenter of the Bruce Landon Award, and Maura Bellamy, presenter of the Kacey Bellamy Girls MVP Award. (Photo by Frederick Gore, The Republican).

Every spare inch in the office of Springfield Mayor Domenic Sarno is filled with photos, memorabilia, books and family photos, many given to him as gifts. This is a Bruce Landon bobblehead, July 25, 2017. (Photo by Don Treeger, The Republican).

Top: From left, Bruce Landon, Bruce Cline, and Yves Locas gather in front of the Eastern States Coliseum on Saturday to celebrate "Hockey day at the Coliseum" on Aug. 10, 2013, an annual gathering of the Springfield Hockey Heritage Society in West Springfield.
(Photo by Dave Roback, The Republican).

Above: The Landon Family at the Hall of Fame event.

INDEX

A
Abrahams, Charles 63
Abrahamsson, Christer 64
Agawam Motor Lodge 37, 44
AHL Hall of Fame 203
Albano, Mike 119, 120, 125
Altieri, Mike 191
Amadio, Dave 34, 165
Anderson, Ed 106, 116, 129
Anderson, Jimmy 38, 42, 160
Andersson, Mikael 92
Andrews, David 108 - 110, 147, 182, 190, 195
Antonucci, Frank 104, 114
Appleby, Ken 134
Avco Cup 63

B
Bailey, Garnet "Ace" 188
Baldwin, Howard 75
Barnett, Mike 171
Barrett, Jeff 124
Barrie, Ontario 33
Baun, Bobby 33
Bavis, Mark 191
Bednar, Jared 158
Beliveau, Jean 27
Bellamy, Maura 210
Bennett, Jim 129, 131
Berry, Bob 82, 161
Bessone Committee 210
Bessone Hockey Awards Banquet 209, 210
Blackburn, Don 149
Blackhawks 187
Blomqvist, Anton 176
bobblehead, Bruce Landon 211
Boddy, Greg 35
Boe, Roy 104
Boston Bruins 59, 82
Boudreau, Bruce "Gabby" 65, 74, 102, 103, 151, 173
Bowman, Scotty 150
Bridge, Don 113
Bridge, Judy 113, 120, 129
Briere, Daniel 171, 172, 186
Brooks, Herb 151, 188, 189
Brown, Andy 33
Bruce Landon Way 7, 15, 201, 204, 206 - 208
Buckberger, Kelly "Bucky" 155
Bullard, Lyman 147
Burgess, Andy 40
Burke, Richard 171
Burke, Taylor 106, 171
Butterfield, Jack 55, 69, 82, 98, 109, 150

215

C

Caffery, Terry 29, 63
Calder Cup 47, 53, 54, 87, 89, 94, 96, 98, 99, 101, 102, 160, 169, 183, 186, 190, 193
Calvanese, Ralph 164-169, 193
Cambi, Joe 119, 120, 128
Cape Cod Codders 74
Carleton, Wayne "Swoop" 75
Carlson, Jack 55, 59, 63, 65, 67, 69, 71, 79, 82, 98, 109, 150, 203
Carlson, Jeff 78, 79
Carlson, Steve 79, 103
Caron, Ron 59
Carpenter, Doug 82
Cavanaugh, Dan 150
Chaput, Michael 136
Chase, Don 118
Chatham Maroons 28
Cheevers, Gerry 75
Chez Paree 100
Chimelis, Ron 10
Chrisanthopoulos, Tracey 207
Cimino, Jonathan 184
Clarkson University 123
Cline, Bruce 160, 212
Columbus Blue Jackets 183
Commentucci, Jim 78
Coogan, Gerry 87, 104
Cooney, Peter 87, 88, 89, 92, 96, 97, 98, 104, 109, 116, 161, 174, 188, 203
Cosell, Howard 128
Costa, Nathan 204, 206
Cote, Roger 165
Craig, Ryan 173, 175
Creighton, Fred 92, 162
Crestview Country Club 133
Cunningham, Skip 75

D

Daum, Rob 155, 156
Day, Joe 96
Demers, Pete 53
Demers, Peter 40

Denver, Jim 40
Desjardins, Gerry 35
Dimauro, Theodore 80
Dineen, Gary 77, 82, 150, 159
Dolgon, Howard 124
Dorey, Jim 74
Dover, John 25
Dryden, Ken 59

E

Eastern States Coliseum 7, 37, 53, 89, 163, 212
Ebright, Thomas 109
Eddie Shore Award 210
Edmonton, Alberta 71
Edmonton Oilers 73, 155, 179, 180
Enfield Twin Rinks 113, 124, 150

F

Fabus, Peter 187
Farrish, Dave 161
Feaster, Jay 181, 182
Flett, Bill "Cowboy" 34
Fusco, Dennis 87, 104

G

Galerstein, Bob 97
Gillis, Paul 150, 155
Gilman, Laurence 130, 186
Gleason, Tim 78
Gordon, Michael 80
Goring, Butch 34
Graham, Dirk 158
Gretzky, Wayne 9, 155, 171
Grills, Paul 28

H

Hackett, Jeff 94, 99
Hall, Glenn 27
Hanna, John 159
Hanson Brothers 78

Harpoon: The Official Magazine of the New England Whalers 70
Harris, Ted 82, 83
Hartford Whalers 64, 98, 150, 186, 187
Harvey, Keith 25
Harvey, Michel 46, 47
Hawks 27
Helmer, Bryan 184, 185
Henning, Lorne 152, 161
Henry, Dale 102
Hoganson, Dale 34
Hoosick Falls 123
Houle, Rejean 30
Howe, Gordie 9, 27, 64, 69
Howson, Scott 182, 185
Hull, Bobby 57, 66
Hurley, Paul 74

I

Isenburg, John 77

J

Jacksonville Barons 71
Janik, Doug 150
Joyce, Eric 147

K

Kacey Bellamy Girls MVP Award 210
Kates, Jason 210
Kellogg, Chris 115
Kelly, Jack 59, 63 - 65, 67, 203
Kilrea, Brian 160
Kingston, Ontario 15, 16, 25, 28, 33, 35, 37, 45, 79, 82, 130, 203
Kingston Frontenacs 82
Kingston, Ontario Hall of Fame 203
Kish, Larry 69, 73
Kurtenbach, Orland 159

L

LaChance, Wayne 13, 111, 118, 122-127, 166, 203

LaForge, Patrick 183
Lamoriello, Lou 130
Landon, Bruce 1, 4, 6-9, 11-12, 14-16, 18, 20, 25, 36, 39-40, 51-52, 65-66, 68, 70, 85, 88, 112-3, 115, 123, 125, 138-140, 143, 150, 154, 169, 175, 180-81, 194, 200-202, 204, 206-212
Landon Family 4, 13, 14, 15, 16, 18, 20, 22, 23, 48, 50, 51, 66, 68, 154, 213
Landon, Jessie Florence May 17
Landon, Marcia 13, 23, 48, 49, 50
Landon, Norm 16
Landon, Tammy Jacobson 2, 3, 5
Landon, Terry 14-15, 17, 19, 21-23, 26-7, 29, 63, 150
Lane, Gordie 74, 159
Larsen, Brad 156, 157
Laycoe, Hal 35
Leary, George 55, 73, 77, 78, 80, 85, 87, 151, 152, 159, 203, 207
Legace, Manny 187, 192
Lemanis, Stephen N. 39, 54
Lemieux, Real "Frenchy" 165
Leroux, Frankie 118
Ley, Rick 69, 74
Locas, Yves 212
Loons, George 40
Los Angeles Kings 31, 33, 34, 35, 40, 43, 44, 77, 115, 123, 172, 179, 191, 203

M

MacFarland, Chris 158, 183, 185
MacGannell, Art 38
Maguire, George 34
Maloney, Don 146
Marion, Chris 134, 194, 198, 200
Massachusetts Hall of Fame 203
MassMutual Center 9, 15, 71, 127, 131, 134, 136, 138, 140, 157, 175, 183, 190, 194, 196, 198, 200-202, 204, 206-208.
McCarthy, Kevin 161
McCormick, Gene 82
McCreary, Bill 160
McDonnell, Terry 150
McLaughlin, Rick 129

McSorley, Marty 155
Miller, Randy 165
Minor Hockey Association 27
Mlakar, Roy 115
Mokosak, John 174
Molnar, David 120, 139, 142, 157, 175, 196
Montreal Canadiens 28, 59, 82
Muckler, John 73
Murray, Mark M. 64, 65, 93, 94, 113, 150, 169, 180
Murray, Rob 142, 166, 167, 169, 172, 186

N

Naismith Memorial Basketball Hall of Fame 181
National Hockey League 28, 29, 35, 61, 158, 173, 181, 183
Neale, Harry 50
Neilson, Roger 29, 30
New England Whalers 13, 44, 59, 61, 66, 70, 72
New York Islanders 46-7, 92, 98, 150, 187

O

Ocampo, Juan 191
Oliver, Bob 117, 124, 128, 131, 142, 144
Oliver, Lena 45, 50, 52
Oliver, Marcia Lee 41
Ontario Hockey League 29

P

Page, Dr. David 172
Pappin, Jim 188
Parks, Greg 103
Patrick, Craig 80, 151
Peterborough Petes 28
Peter Pan Bus 37, 195
Phoenix Coyotes 130, 171
Picknelly, Paul 195, 199, 208
Picknelly, Peter A. 37, 112-3, 128
Picknelly Sr., Peter 114, 119
Pittsburgh Penguins 31, 63, 130

Plante, Jacques 33
Pollock, Sam 82
Pompea, Charlie 13, 133, 138, 139, 140, 143, 148
Pompea, Sarah 138
Pompei, Sam 40, 82
Pope Francis High School 209
Portland Pirates 109, 147, 198
Potvin, Marc 154
Price, Noel 39
Pro Friends Inc. 106, 119, 121
Providence Bruins 106, 136
Pulford, Bob 187
Puppolo, Angelo 206

R

Reason, Bill "Squeak" 28
Regan, Larry 34, 40, 203
Republican, The 39, 52, 54, 64-5, 69, 78, 80, 90, 92-3, 96, 101, 108, 112-3, 115, 120, 122, 125, 136, 139-140, 142-3, 150-3, 157, 164, 167, 169, 171, 175, 180-4, 190, 192, 194, 196, 199-202, 204, 206-212.
Riley, Rob 156
Roback, Dave 92, 115, 136, 143, 152, 202, 204, 206, 207, 208, 212
Roberts, Jimmy 93, 96, 99, 100, 103-4, 149
Roberts, Tom 114
Rob Murray Award 142
Roethweiller, John 77
Rokowski, Brian 142
Rolfe, Dale 34
Rousseau, Dunc 53
Ruuska, Seppo 28
Ryan, Ron 75

S

Sacenti, Richard 178
Samuelsson, Henrik 134
Sanderson, Derek 57
Sapelli, William 210
Sarno, Domenic J. 115, 206, 208
Screech 196, 198

Segall, Michelle 96
Selwood, Brad 51, 74
Shack, Eddie 44
Shore, Bob 210
Shore, Eddie 77, 160, 163, 164, 165, 210
Shuman, Phil 114, 133
Sinden, Harry 80, 82, 162
Smith, Al 63, 64, 74
Smith, Billy 43, 45, 46, 47, 59
Smith, Floyd 160
Smith, Oliver 19
Sneddon, Bob 42
Springfield Falcons 9, 13, 76, 104-106, 111-115, 117-119, 123-124, 134-139, 142, 145, 150, 155-157, 161, 164, 166, 168-170, 175, 180-187, 192, 196, 198, 201-202
Springfield Foodservice Corp. 120
Springfield Hockey Heritage Society 212
Springfield Indians 42, 52, 69, 74, 80, 82, 87, 89, 90, 92, 93, 94, 96, 101, 117, 152
Springfield Kings 7, 13, 36, 37, 38, 39, 40, 47, 54, 71
Springfield Kings Hockey Magazine 36, 38
Springfield Olympia 124
Springfield Thunderbirds 9, 190, 201, 204
Stackhouse, Ron 29, 31
Stanley Cup 63, 174, 187
Stelleck, Gord 103
Stemkowski, Pete 154
Stemkowski, Peter 82, 154, 159
Stevens, John 166, 172
Stirling, Steve 159
St. Louis Blues 104
Suchocki, John 69
Svedberg, Niklas 136
Sweeney, Bill 160
Sweet, Mike 129

T
Tardiff, Marc 30
The Student Prince 115
Thompson, Chris 200
Toronto Maple Leafs 63, 74, 130, 161, 179, 187
Toropchenko, Leonid 177
Torrey, Bill 92, 99, 150
Treeger, Don 92, 164, 184, 190, 199, 201, 211
Truitt, Jeff 155
Tuohey, David 210
Turley Publications 106
Turley, Tom 106

V
Victoria, British Columbia 43

W
Webster, Tom 74, 81, 151
Whidden, Bob 74
Whitmore, Kay 92, 99
Wilkes-Barre, Pennsylvania 124
Williams, Tommy 74
Wilson, John 153
Wilson, Johnny 42, 46, 55, 163
Wood, Lyman 112, 113, 119, 128, 199

Z
Zaranek, Ben 209

NOTES

NOTES

NOTES

NOTES

NOTES